STARTING A BUSINESS

THE 15 RULES FOR A SUCCESSFUL BUSINESS

Text Copyright © Mark Atwood

All rights reserved. No part of this guide may be reproduced in any form without permission in writing from the publisher except in the case of brief quotations embodied in critical articles or reviews.

Legal & Disclaimer

The information contained in this book and its contents is not designed to replace or take the place of any form of medical or professional advice; and is not meant to replace the need for independent medical, financial, legal or other professional advice or services, as may be required. The content and information in this book has been provided for educational and entertainment purposes only.

The content and information contained in this book has been compiled from sources deemed reliable, and it is accurate to the best of the Author's knowledge, information and belief. However, the Author cannot guarantee its accuracy and validity and cannot be held liable for any errors and/or omissions. Further, changes are periodically made to this book as and when needed. Where appropriate and/or necessary, you must consult a professional (including but not limited to your doctor, attorney, financial advisor or such other professional advisor) before using any of the suggested remedies, techniques, or information in this book.

Upon using the contents and information contained in this book, you agree to hold harmless the Author from and against any damages, costs, and expenses, including any legal fees potentially resulting from the application of any of the information provided by this book. This disclaimer applies to any loss, damages or injury caused by the use and application, whether directly or indirectly, of any advice or information presented, whether for breach of contract, tort, negligence, personal injury, criminal intent, or under any other cause of action. You agree to accept all risks of using the information presented inside this book.

You agree that by continuing to read this book, where appropriate and/or necessary, you shall consult a professional (including but not limited to your doctor, attorney, or financial advisor or such other advisor as needed) before using any of the suggested remedies, techniques, or information in this book

Table of Contents

Introduction 1

Chapter 1: Essentials For A Successful Business Startup 4

Chapter 2: The Business Planning Process Step By Step 7

Chapter 3: The True Meaning Of Business 10

Chapter 4: Incorporation - How To Maximize Benefits 14

Chapter 5: The Starting Point For Your Business - What Most People Ignore And Then Fail 19

Chapter 6: 10 Mindsets That Will Radically Improve Your Business 22

Chapter 7: What Is Business Law - Protect Yourself And Avoid Overnight Bankrupcy 29

Chapter 7.1: Understanding Trademarks And Copyright 32

Chapter 8: Marketing - Get Noticed & Scale Up Rapidly 38

Chapter 9: The 4ps And Web Marketing 43

Chapter 10: Known And Unknown Ways To Grow Your Business Into A Million-Dollar Corporation 67

Chapter 11: Effective Use Social Media For Incredible Expansion & Growth 83

Chapter 12: Six Critical Game-Changing Business Habits 93

Chapter 13: Why Do People Fail In Business & How Can You Avoid Total Failure? 96

Chapter 14: 7 Proven Ways To Turn Past Failures Into Success 102

Chapter 15: Establishing Customer Relations Through Effective Communication To Maximize Profits 110

Conclusion 124

Introduction

Thank you for your purchase. Your investment in this book will be well worth it. The value you are going to receive from this resource is going to help you in business for a lifetime. Every bit of content is up-to-date and high quality. What you are going to read is based on my own and the experience and success of many other great businessmen and women. This book was not written out of boredom or to make more money. Sure, I might get a tiny bit of extra income but that will probably not even affect my total income by a fraction. I am successful and I have achieved my financial goals. Now I am here to share my knowledge and expertise for you to achieve your dreams!

I'm pretty sure you've searched lots of websites like Amazon and other similar ones in order to grab a book that teaches the best strategies to start up a business and due to your attainment, you've been worried about who you should trust. You have chosen the right guy to listen to.

Business is not for everyone. It takes a lot of work and struggles to create a successful business and you are probably already aware of this. Nevertheless, if you're persistent enough and willing to be exposed to the business world in order to start a successful business, you shouldn't be carried away some minor problems and hardships. Don't get discouraged, keep on going and never give up!

They're lots of people who're not experienced and write books on various topics which they don't have any experience about. You need someone who is experienced, someone who has tried out a lot already and have gotten all the way-out to various circumstances who will effectively teach you the necessary basics and which you can easily get help from when needed.

Luckily, you have me. Should we call it luck or not? Actually no, it is not luck. You made a decision and bought this book out of your own will. One of the first steps to achieving something great in business or any other kind of endeavor is to do something about it such as getting educated. By purchasing this book, you have proven to yourself that you are willing to make a change and I respect you for that. The majority will not even get this far.

I have been a businessman since my early twenties and I have ventured into so many businesses and failed countless time, however, there's a saying; *"I have not failed. I've just found 10,000 ways that won't work."* - Thomas A. Edison. This saying motivated me a lot at the initial stages of my business career. At the beginning, it is very usual to make a lot of mistakes (ask any successful person), however, I never saw a mistake or a failure as defeat or a reason to quit. I saw every tiny error as a learning opportunity to grow and be better until the next time. This is a major difference between the those who fail miserably and quit and those who achieve great things and gets to the top. Those who don't make it see their failures as lost battles that they are unable to come back from. Successful people, however, take the hit, might even lose the first battle but comes back for more in the next war.

Starting up a business takes more than just a good idea and motivation, you also need to be persistent and positive. You need to go about it with a strong mindset, don't expect an overnight miracle and always remember it's a business and it is supposed to be difficult.

I'm sure you don't want an average life, your dream is bigger than that. I had similar thoughts when I was new to the arena but I made sure that I was going to make it. I did not want to work for someone else for the rest of my life and be like one of those miserable, grumpy old men and women who complain about everything and everyone.

Educate yourself, stay determined and no matter what happens, keep your head up and keep on going!

Chapter 1:

Essentials For A Successful Business Startup

One main problem when first starting a business is the need for startup capital. You have probably heard that you have to spend money in order to make money. This is somewhat true, but only if you actually have the money to spend. Putting money inside of a startup fund when you do not have money is obviously difficult. The startup cost can look to be unachievable and even daunting. Unfortunately, business startup capital is one of the chief things that keep people from starting a business in the first place. There are, however, several organizations and individual investors that could help you with the startup costs. You may apply for a bank loan or present your idea to an investor and hopefully receive the capital you need in exchange for interest payments or losing a percentage of the company ownership. You also have to remember that there are several billion dollar companies today such as HP that have started with a startup fund of under $1000. Any barrier can be overcome if you put your mind to it.

At first, bank loans might be hard to get. Banking establishments usually prefer to give out loans to companies that can show some kind of revenue and profit. Also, banks do want a foolproof industry program, which can be challenging for someone who is starting his small business for the first time. Fortunately, you have other ways to search for business startup capital.

Business startup funding for small business is not only a hindrance in the way of an enterpriser from starting a trade, but also can obstruct growing of an new enterprise. On top of being a problem at the start, having limited startup funds can also make it difficult to hire employees or get sufficient stocks.

New trade seekers can also decide to apply for several companies that are offering small trade loans to aid people get the necessary startup capital. There is one good company which is called "American One", offering unbarred loans for assistance to small entrepreneurs for starting their business. They specialize with business startup costs and understand the hardships of trying to set it up and they work hard to make the procedure simple and easy.

Some entrepreneurs seek out business partners to assist them with their small business startup price. A investing partner can supply you with the essential assistance needed for a small trade startups. They can run as "silent partner" where they just contribute their investment money and then have their commission paid based on the partnership agreement. Other investing partners are more than involved and might aid in the operation of the trade in order to ensure that their business investment is profitable and well managed. Private investors might also ask to own a percentage meaning that they would be a part owner. A tip here is to always keep at least %51 of the company to yourself. The one individual with the most number of shares of the company has the most control as well.

Since small trade business is really the backbone of world economic system, several government authorities offer a mixture of programs to aid startup business organizations become successful in their endeavor. This is important since small industry startup investment value is a primary ground that most clever people with superb ideas do not get their trade started. Banks can be unapproachable to small industry businessmen, but they also have other options such as functioning with companies who build the procedure easier and less stressful for businessmen. As an event, many individuals have gotten their dreams true and achieved successfully by operating and starting their very own small business.

A startup cost is a barrier to entry. The barrier to entry can obviously vary a lot from depending on which industry or what type of company we are talking about. A lot of people view this barrier to entry as a huge problem, however, that is completely wrong.Why? The barrier of entry filters out the weak minded people which equals less competition for you and less competition equals more customers coming to you.

Chapter 2:

The Business Planning Process Step By Step

Business planning is one of the most important steps towards building a successful business, and you can use some specific strategies to create a comprehensive outline. A effective business plan will help you determine your goals and help you organize all of your small business ideas with ease. If you've ever been stuck with too many ideas and not knowing where to start, business planning will help take the pressure off. Understanding the business planning process is important for creating something that works, and something that will help you reach your goals. Launching your small business is much easier with a clear, step-by-step outline; here's what you need to know:

Step 1: Organize your table of contents. This will help you outline each area of your business to include your mission statement, products and services, number of employees, and any basic market research information.

Step 2: Collect attachments and appendix materials. These are especially important if your business plan will be reviewed by potential investors or business partners, and can also help with your online business planning strategy.

Step 3: Create a list of key topics and sections. Not only will this create a cohesive document, but you'll also be able to jumpstart your business planning process with a clear 'map' or guide of all your strategies. This list is especially helpful if you're not sure where to begin, since you can just put each item down on paper and organize it accordingly.

Step 4: Assign projects and tasks for each area. This is an effective business planning strategy as it helps you break down each goal into actions steps. Assigning tasks and objectives in this way makes it much easier to stay on track during each step.

Step 5: Check for grammar, spelling, and even factual errors. Making sure your plan and notes are clear of mistakes is especially important if you'll be presenting it to others. Doing a quick check will also help you determine if you missed any pieces of critical information and help you fine tune the final draft.

Step 6: Write up an executive summary for your business startup. This is a important step for all business owners, and can help you pull together the entire plan in a few short pages. Many business owners turn to this summary when they need a briefing on objectives during the course of business, and you can include basic points and topics as if you were presenting it to a board or audience.

Step 7: Get an outsider's perspective. While you need to keep your business planning strategy and ideas as confidential as possible, sharing your plan with a trustworthy person can help you catch a few key elements of your project. Get a objective view of your plan and notes so you have everything in well-organized and presented in a logical way.

Business planning doesn't have to be difficult, but many startup business owners are intimidated by the process. Take the time to organize the critical areas of your business and put them in a logical order. Then, break them down into specific objectives and tasks so you have a strong idea of how you can be successful in each area. The time and effort you put into business planning will pay off for the long run and help you launch your business with success.

Chapter 3:

The True Meaning Of Business

Business should be defined as an activity which provides needed goods and services at a profit to the people. How would you define business? Before you accept the standard definition, pose these questions to yourself and others:

1. The definition above states that a business engages in selling "needed" goods to society. Is this always true? Is there a difference between something needed and something wanted? Do people need and want things based on their own value system or do businesses create needs and wants through advertising? Are cigarettes a need, a want, or a business created desire?

2. What about illegal goods? Society, in general, doesn't want marijuana to exist yet we have people that sell it at a profit to a segment or target group in our society who desire it. Is something not a business because it sells illegal goods?

3. Is business always conducted to turn a profit? Some entities sell but not with the objective of earning a monetary profit. The Democratic and Republican parties in The United States sell candidates to the American public. The objective is not an immediate monetary profit but a gain of power and influence. Do you agree that the

selling of a candidate and political party's ideas are a type of product or service?

4. What about non-profit organizations? Some organizations are designed to provide goods and services but not for a profit. When a local restaurant opens and makes a profit, it pays taxes and retains part or all of the aftertax profits in the business. The increase in the firm's assets (such as cash or restaurant equipment) is listed on the books of the company as having come from retained earnings. The firm will often reward those who made the business successful with higher salaries or bonuses in addition to retaining some of the profits to expand the firm. If a local non-profit hospital makes excess money, it doesn't pay taxes on the profit, it simply retains the entire amount as a surplus. Similar to the successful restaurant, the hospital will also reward the people that made it a success with higher salaries or bonuses, and/or use its surplus retained money to expand its services. Do you agree that in many situations, the only difference between making a profit in a business and achieving surplus earnings in a non-profit business is that one pays income tax and the other does not?

There is another important difference between profit-seeking firms and non-profit organizations such as political parties or community-sponsored hospitals. Profit-seeking firms have owners. Non-profit firms have a governing body so no one "owns" the firm.

Ownership is of key importance in many aspects of a for-profit business. Of course, for-profit and non-profit businesses have much in common. Both profit and non-profit businesses must seek start-up capital (money to buy inventory, machinery, ambulances, fixtures, etc.). Both types of organizations are held accountable to the individuals or groups that provided the start-up money. Both must seek continual revenues to stay in business. All profit firms must find a service or product that the market will purchase.

Non-profit businesses must do the same and/or appeal to donors in order to stay in business. Non-profit businesses are sometimes faced with the interesting, dual marketing problem of how to provide services or products to meet a need while simultaneously convincing a second market (donors) that they should provide funds. Consequently, nonprofit businesses must carefully monitor two very different markets (the benefactors of the service or product and the donors).

Consider the additional information regarding for-profit owners and not-for-profit governing boards. In defining "What is a Business" should a distinction be made between for-profit and not-for-profit businesses?

Risk and Return:

The knowledge you will gain about business in this book can be applied to almost all organizations and institutions in the world. By definition, they all have one thing in common. A business is an enterprise where the owners, boards or managers takes risk in order to make a profit, gain excess earnings, secure power, influence the lives of others, gain prestige, or ensure self-preservation. This is what business is about: Taking a risk in order to gain a return (risk and return). If you take a risk expecting on average to lose, it's called gambling. If on the other hand, you take a risk expecting on average to gain it's called an investment.

Chapter 4:

Incorporation - How To Maximize Benefits

A governmental authority administers incorporation. In the United States, incorporation is a state process, not a national or federal process. States have varied incorporation requirements with some states being pro-business. Other states seem more interested in protecting investors and keeping a close watch over firms rather than making it easy for businesses to incorporate. Incorporation is not a complicated process even when states are not pro-business nor is it expensive.

Why do businesses incorporate? Once incorporated the firm assumes the legal status of an individual. This provides the owners or executives personal protection. If, for example, a firm makes a serious mistake or an accident occurs a lawsuit may result. The lawsuit will be directed at the corporation rather than the owners and managers. In some cases, where their was intent to do harm or prudent decision making was not used, certain officials in the corporation might be included in the lawsuit.

With legal protection provided, stock investors, are more likely to write a check to the firm and become part owner of the business. When the investors want to get out of the business the legal protection through incorporation makes it easier for the original investor to find a new investor that will write a check for the stock. It is important that you note the firm only receives money from the original sale of the stocks and is not involved in the future resale or exchange of the stock between investors.

Investors also like the idea that if one investor has personal, health, legal, or financial problems, it does not directly affect the firm. Each investor can exit when they want to simply by finding some new investor that will buy the stock from them. The new investor assumes the same rights of the investor that sold the stock. Therefore, the remaining shareholders do not care who holds the shares of stock.

Other forms of business ownership are often used. A person or a husband and wife might start a business by taking out a business license from their city, county or provincial government agency in charge. Sole proprietorships are very easy to start and are often done for small sized businesses. However, proprietorships do not provide for additional owners to join and supply management talent and/or additional funds.

If the business needs more than one owner in order to get the needed funds or human resource assets (programmer, mechanic, ER medical doctor, etc.) then a partnership form of organization can be set up. Partners can join by adding capital and/or talent. While the excitement of working with a partner overcomes many team management problems, eventually most partnerships refer back to their legal partnership agreement to settle disputes.

Another benefit of corporations over sole proprietorships and partnerships as a legal business entity is that individual investors can sell their interest in the firm (shares of stock) without disrupting the firm itself. Thus, if investors become irritated with the firm's performance or they need money quickly they can sell their stock to another individual. The corporation does not repurchase the stock. Thus, ownership continues to change but the corporation maintains the funds from the original sale of stock and the management team stays intact.

Think of it as General Motors selling you a new car. GM has your money and you have the car. When you sell your car, GM does not repurchase it. Instead, the sale will be made to a car dealer or a private party.

When investors decide to sell their stock, they can advertise the stock in the classified advertisement section of a newspaper. It is rare, but sometimes that is the only method to find a stock buyer if the company is a little, regional firm. Selling the stock of small, regional firms is a difficult process since buyers cannot be easily located. If by luck, a buyer is found, determining the value of a share in a business is not easy, even when both buyer and seller bargain in good faith for a fair value. It is difficult to come to an agreement over the price of an automobile, which is tangible and is parked right in front of the buyer and seller. How much is a piece of paper worth that has rights to partial ownership in a business?

A system has been developed to facilitate the buying and selling of "used" stocks. There are famous names in the business of bringing stock buyers and sellers together such as the New York Stock Exchange (NYSE), the American Stock Exchange (AMEX) and the National Association of Securities Dealers Automated Quotations (NASDAQ). Before one of these large stock exchanges will handle the resale of a stock in a firm, that firm must have achieved some positive investment reputation. The firm must have enough shares and numerous stockholders, such that every day one could expect buy and sell orders for shares of stock.

The process of examining a firm to see if it meets the requirements for active trading in the large stock exchanges is called **Listing**. If an exchange determines that the volume of trading will generate sufficient revenue for the exchange and, that the firm agrees to make certain financial data public, the stock is listed.

Having a stock "listed" or traded allows the investors to quickly and easily find a buyer for their stock. The ability to change an asset, such as a stock, quickly into cash without having to lower the price is called **Liquidity**. Cash is the ultimate in liquidity.

Stock on a listed exchange is quite liquid (you might take a loss on what you paid for it, but you will get the cash for what it is worth that day). A non-listed stock like a used car is less liquid. A home is generally a great asset but is not very liquid. Depending on the market, homes might turnover (sell) in three months but in some cases it might take 12 months or more. The more liquid the asset, the easier to take care of adjustments in your personal life and the easier to move from one investment to a better one. Liquidity provides options.

Chapter 5:

The Starting Point For Your Business - What Most People Ignore And Then Fail

People organize to achieve some goal or objective. It might be a simple short-run goal such as a surprise party. It might be a very long run complex plan such as establishing plants, equipment and a marketing force to dominate the world auto market.

Before you can navigate, you need to know where you want to go. Where you want to go is referred to as your intent or vision. Entrepreneurs create a vision of where they want to go, develop a plan to get there and then proceed. Sometimes, the vision is based on a new piece of equipment, idea, or invention they came up with by being involved with another task. Something as simple as a home baked cookie in the hands of an entrepreneur with a vision can become a $100,000,000 business.

The Starting Point for Your Team:

Your business team will be asked to establish a vision statement. Each member of the team needs to participate in the creation of that vision statement. The statement can be based on several standards. Do you want your firm to end the simulation with a value created for the stockholder that exceeds the value created by any other team? Or, would you like the value your team created to be in the upper half of all firms? These two visions based on the same standard are very different. Each requires the team to consider how the firm is financed, how assets are used, how to react to competitors and how hard the team will work. Desiring to be the best also requires the team to take on more risk than most firms in order to achieve above average gains. As in most business ventures, taking on more risk exposes the team to a greater chance of failure.

Returns to stockholders can be measured by the simulation's standardized assessment system which evaluates the original value a stockholder put in (cost of one share of stock) against the last average annual price of the stock plus any dividends. Another more simple measure provided by the simulation is the rate of annual profit when measured against the stockholder's total investment. A return on the stockholder's investment (their total equity) of 15% is far better than a return of 8%. A firm can measure itself easily against the return on equity of all the other firms in the simulation.

Creating value for stockholders is one standard. Another common performance standard is sales. Your team might go into business with the intent to achieve more sales annually than any other firm in the simulation. This vision of being the largest sales organization in the simulation will require dependable finished goods suppliers, a large capital structure, close monitoring of the competition (in your industry and in other industries), and an aggressive well-defined marketing program.

If you don't like the performance standards of creating value for stockholders or annual sales, what about profit after tax? Suppose you were to measure profit after tax. The team could measure the firm's total annual profits against competitors but the larger firms tend to have the larger amounts of profits. Therefore, measure profits as a percentage of assets. Then you are measuring management's skill at utilizing the assets they have in their control. A return of 20% annually on assets is better than a 15% return regardless of the firm's size. With the highest return on assets (sometimes called return on total investment, both debt and equity) the team can then say: "We are the best run firm in the industry."

Chapter 6:

10 Mindsets That Will Radically Improve Your Business

Success is something all career-driven individuals desire yet it eludes many people -- at least at the levels desired. Why are some businesspeople successful and others not?

It has everything to do with habits, beliefs, passion, flexibility, and attitude.

Often there's nothing really different between one entrepreneur and another in term of ability, as each person can do whatever he or she wants. What it all comes down to is having the frame of mind to set practical habits and keep a balance between attachment and commitment and letting things happen.

Here are 10 mindsets for success:

1. Choose courage over fear.

To be successful, you must have courage and in order to become courageous, you must do courageous things. Much of being successful is about going beyond what you think you're capable of venturing into the unknown. Whether you fail or succeed, you will learn and grow.

Growth, in and of itself, means attaining a level of success whether it came from success or failure.

2. Believe in yourself.

Attitude is everything. A negative attitude decreases success and a positive attitude creates success. Without that belief in yourself, you'll lack a path to success.

Success is something that's created. It's not something that merely "happens."

When you firmly believe in yourself, you can achieve virtually anything: It's within this belief that you'll find the power to create the resilience and fortitude needed to keep going when things get tough.

3. Choose good company.

Whom you surround yourself with is among the most important choices you'll make as you climb up the business ladder. Negativity is contagious and if work groups and/or leaders, are negative there will be a ceiling to your success.

To reach the goals you desire, be willing to change bosses if necessary. Or if you're the boss, rid your team of toxic people immediately.

It only takes one toxic person to destroy the morale of an entire campaign. Further, when you surround yourself with other successful, goal-oriented individuals, you can learn from them and take on some of their habits to add to your own as you proceed along your road to success.

Always remember that you are the equivalent of the five people you spend the most time with.

4. Adopt self-chosen goals.

Knowing and being clear about where you're headed in business is something that must come from within. When your goals selected by you, you're more motivated to achieve them.

That's because by achieving these goals, you attain a new desired piece of yourself. When your goals arise from your instigation, they carry a deeper meaning and confer a greater impact on your identity.

Each self-selected goal realized adds a depth and an internal expansion to you as a person. Personal expansion is just one of the great gifts to come from succeeding in your business goals.

5. Have a purpose and a vision.

Visualization is powerful because actions follow thoughts. A great technique for nurturing your vision and purpose is to make your goals visual. Some people use vision boards; others opt for treasure maps. And still others set goals identifying specific dates for their achievement.

Whatever works best is a matter for the individual to figure out.

I believe that anything that's written down is more likely to be achieved. Having visions and goals just in your head is not the most effective way to set the path for success. When you make your purpose visual, you make it real. When you keep them in your mind, they remain wishes.

6. Accept the challenge.

There are few easy paths up a mountain and often they're hard to find. Overcoming challenges are an essential piece in any type of success in business.

Challenge is what creates your growth along the journey. Each challenge obstructing your path provides you with the chance to create a more defined direction toward attaining your dream vendors, customers, managers, employees -- and numbers. For this reason, bless each challenge. Each one is a compass directing you toward new business leads, circumstances and opportunities.

7. Be discerning.

Selectivity creates success. You must think deeply and intelligently about the bigger picture and what it is you need for each step along the way to continue articulating and executing your business goals.

Mindfulness means being aware of all angles and staying sharply in touch with the present so that you do not have to clean up mistakes in the future.

Be discerning of group dynamics: which person is the best at what job, which customers or deals will take you the furthest and what it is that each moment is calling on you to do or change to be the most efficient.

That's how selectivity offers you the pursuit of success.

8. Be willing to take risks.

There are no guarantees on any path to success in life or business. The unknown is always looming. Therefore, risk and education are often the mechanisms necessary for knowing more clearly if you're on the right path.

If you're afraid to risk, you will put limits on your success and stay where you're comfortable. You cannot get what you want if you don't risk rejection and go for what you desire.

9. Do what you love.

You're more likely to succeed in business when you're invested in your passion and making your career fit your personality.

There is a way to find passion about anything and everything you do in life.

You may not love every part of your job but tolerating discomforts by looking at the bigger picture makes your investment of time and energy worthwhile.

Be willing to love and find purpose in all aspects of what your business requires, commit to it and see what you're doing as being a benefit to others. When you love the business you're in, there is nothing that can keep you from wanting to work at it, nurture it and make it grow.

10. Gratitude.

When you see life and career in terms of the lack in what you have achieved, you cannot drive your business up the ladder of success. Then negativity is impeding your progress.

You must look at all you have and realize how great what you have is as compared to the situation of many others.

When you have this attitude, you stop suffering and complaining about the small stuff. On each receipt you pay out, write thank you. That's not only to thank the person, event, vendor or customer for what's provided you but also to give a private thanks acknowledging that you have the abundance necessary to pay for the service, product or event.

Habits coupled with flexibility provide you with a path to success. Success is fluid and so rigidity will stand in its way.

Developing these mindsets give you a compass to navigate the ever-changing tides on the way to business and financial goals. These mindsets allow openness and flexibility while also providing you precise direction.

Chapter 7:

What Is Business Law - Protect Yourself And Avoid Overnight Bankrupcy

Everything that relates to our society is governed by laws and business is no exception. Business law or commercial law is simply a body of law that governs every aspect with regards to conducting a business. This covers but not limited to the commerce of the sea, transportation of goods, guarantees, marine life and natural disasters pertaining to the economic status and business relations, life of the people concerned, employment, intellectual property, insurances and conformities of partnerships. Business may differ for each state or country but there are international codes followed to ensure equal distribution of economic power among nations.

In some countries, civil codes that cover comprehensive statements of their commercial law are being followed. They are usually regulated by the congress with its power to regulate interstate commerce. In the United States, unions are formed to promote a uniform body of commercial law which has resulted in the adoption of the uniform commercial code which is currently being followed by the 50 states and other US territories.

Business law is applicable to both small and big. With its broad coverage, several branches of it are categorized to avoid confusion and to promote formality in the process. One of these branches of law is the advertising law. This law ensures that products are being advertised truthfully and to protect the consumers from false promises. Another notable law is the employment and labor law. This law protects the employees working for a firm. This includes health insurances, discrimination and harassment protection, child labor, household employment, posters, employment termination, wage and hour laws, final paychecks and compensation for work. Business law also has its own set of finance law that protects all scale of business establishments. This helps small firms from the harassment of big companies and to level the ground of competition and promote a healthy market. There is also a law that protects and governs online businesses. This covers the financial and legal liabilities incurred in the areas of privacy, security, taxation and copyright issues. Business law also includes a set of environmental regulations. All businesses are required to follow a set of rules and regulations when affecting the natural environment. Any harm done to the environment is not permitted except in some rare cases. Employee's healthy and safety is also covered by the law.

Before you start your own business, you should always familiarize yourself with the different laws to avoid legal liabilities and to protect yourself from fraudulent attacks. A strong understanding of the laws will reflect the way you handle your business and will eventually determine your success.

Chapter 7.1:

Understanding Trademarks and Copyright

How does the Intellectual Property Office relate to your business? Well, it can help you protect it - namely protect your business name and image from theft.

Copyright law is one thing, it's 'automatic' in the United Kingdom with no need to officially register it, and offers you a certain measure of ownership to your company name and logo design/company identity, but it's not quite as firm and definite as an official 'trademark', and this is what the Intellectual Property Office can offer you.

First and foremost, what is "copyright"?

In the UK Copyright is automatic for fixed works (does not cover 'ideas'), and this includes photographs, audio recordings of books, paintings and other artwork, writing and more. A business or individual does not need to apply for copyright - it is automatically applied to anything they create.

Examples of works covered automatically by copyright include novels, instruction manuals, computer programs, lyrics, dramatic works, drawings, logos, layouts, broadcasts, and more.

It is illegal to copy or use work protected by copyright without the owner's permission.

Thus if you are a company with a logo design, it's safe to a large extent in that it's automatically copyrighted and you simply need to ensure that whoever created the logo for you, is passing on full copyright ownership to yourself and this is stated in their terms and conditions (of hiring them) or that you are provided with a copyright assignment document for your design.

If someone were to attempt to 'copy' or use your logo design, you would simply need to advise them of their illegality and tell them to cease their activity. If they refuse (rare), you are then in the position of deciding whether to take this to a court, and to win your case you need to prove you are the copyright owner to this design.

When you have registered the trademark to your design, you've already proved it, and this is where the difference lies.

I will explain what the TM and R symbols mean in relation to business trademarking when you see them applied to logo designs; who can and cannot use them - because the distinction is quite important, for instance it's illegal to use the TM symbol unless your business is a 'registered' trademark.

TM Symbol

When you see this common small two letter symbol it tells us that the business owner is using that company name, and/or accompanying logo design icon as a company trade mark, it does not mean that their logo design trade mark has actually been legally 'registered'.

Thus any business can use the trade mark symbol next to their company logo. Doing so helps to establish what is called 'common law' trade mark rights which will offer some degree of protection.

With common law you can potentially stop someone from using your trade mark if you can evidence that;

- The mark/name is yours
- You have built up a business reputation using this mark/name
- The other person's use of your mark harms your business.

This is called 'passing off' and can be a very difficult and expensive procedure. By registering your mark, taking legal action becomes much simpler.

R Symbol

The ® symbol (letter R encased in a circle) is a trademark registration symbol and the distinction between this and the TM symbol is very important. The R symbol can only be used alongside a company logo design once that mark had been applied for and actually legally registered as a trade mark, affording the owner of the mark a lot more protection. To use this symbol when your mark has not be registered is an offence.

Having your company name registered as a Ltd company at Companies House does not mean that you have registered a trade mark for your company name and/or symbol.

Registering your trade mark gives you the exclusive right to use your mark for the goods and/or services that it covers in the United Kingdom, and by putting the ® symbol alongside your company logo design warns others against using it.

It also allows you to take legal action against anyone who uses your mark without your permission and if you win your case Trading Standards Officers or Police are able to bring criminal charges against them.

A registered trade mark is your property, which means you can sell it or allow people to use it by licencing it.

What Can You Register

Any application to register your trade mark must be for a name and/or symbol which is distinctive for the goods and/or services you provide.

An example would be that if you sell eggs you can't register the trade mark name "eggs" because that is just a general name for your product which is used by all and is not distinctive for your company only.

You could however apply to register something like Fresh Eggs Direct, or Southgate Eggs

What Can't You Register

- You can't describe your products/services for your trade mark. As mentioned above... you can't apply to trade mark 'eggs' just because you sell eggs.
- Protected emblems such as official signs or crests, or 3D shapes that are typical of the goods/services you offer.
- Marks/names that are offensive or against the law, or promote drugs etc.
- Deceptive names/marks that seek to mislead the public.

Is It Mine Forever Once Registered?

Once registered your trade mark will be in force for 10 years, after which time, you will be permitted to apply to renew your trade mark for a further ten years... and so on...

How to Register Your Trademark

Many business owners use a trademark lawyer to register their trademark for them, however if you feel it is unlikely you will be 'challenged' (another firm challenges your application by citing that their own mark is the same/too similar), it is simple, and relatively low cost to make the application yourself and you can even do this online.

Chapter 8:

Marketing - Get Noticed & Scale Up Rapidly

Most of your marketing experiences have been as a buyer. Think about how many items you purchased in retail stores during your lifetime. What is your first recollection of a purchase? Probably grabbing something at the grocery store while your mother attempted to keep you under control. How does it happen that a buyer can go to the grocery store and find items to buy at an acceptable price? Who made what decisions to places orange juice just where you need it, at the time you need it, at the price you can afford, and tell you about it?

How do marketing systems in a nation come to be? People have a need for a product and have been informed about the product through the firm's promotion of that product. The customer requires that the product or service be in some geographic place and available within some narrowly defined time period. Of course, this must all take place at a price the buyer is willing to pay. These requirements to meet a buyer's needs are often referred to as the "4 P's" of marketing:

- Product
- Place

- Price
- Promotion.

How the 4P's are implemented in a nation depends in large part on how society sets up its infrastructure. Infrastructure is the physical support structure that moves things from place to place in a society. The "things" being moved about could be people, products, voice, video, water, electricity, data, letters, parcels, raw materials, etc.. Because of the enormous scale (size) of building infrastructure within a nation, the government generally undertakes the project or provides legal and financial support to private enterprises to encourage firms to take on the needed projects. Examples of such projects would be roads, canals, dams, railroads, post offices, airports, and telecommunication systems.

Sometimes governments actually operate enterprises tied closely to infrastructure projects. Examples would be electrical generating plants (hydraulic, fossil fuel, and nuclear), phone systems, toll roads, waste management systems, and mail delivery.

If a country's population is widely scattered and roads are poor, catalog sales may be the method by which the population fills most of their needs for non-perishable goods.

If the government subsidizes (covers part of the cost) of the mail system, even more, catalog sales will occur. As households in a society become more concentrated, government revenues increase for that area allowing roads to be built. Infrastructure is not consistently distributed throughout any one political or geographic area. It is known that efficiencies in manufacturing and distribution are gained as infrastructure improvements are made. The efficiencies lower the cost of goods to consumers and increase profits to businesses creating additional wealth within the society.

The Internet is a new infrastructure system that is changing all aspects of marketing. The Internet system was initially a government-sponsored infrastructure project utilizing privately owned telephone lines. Its purpose was for defense, not commercial use. Once the infrastructure was in place, however, commercial applications followed. Virtual retail stores that sell products and services directly to consumers on the Internet are now common.

Southwest Airlines in the United States, for example, is making it convenient to shop for and purchase tickets on the Internet, thus bypassing an entire travel agency industry. Other market-oriented firms are considering the Internet as a means to promote their products.

Society, through its government's sponsorship or encouragement, creates the infrastructure, which allows for the development of business and the marketing of its goods and services. Society, through its government, also creates rules and regulations that dictate how private firms can use and develop the infrastructure. For example, a government can make it illegal for any firm to compete with its own postal service or it can allow limited competition from private carriers such as DHL or United Parcel Service.

It is important that the members of a society understand the importance of creating infrastructure and the government's direct and indirect role in this process. Good infrastructure will permit the creation of wealth and opportunity for many people within that society.

Entrepreneurs in poor nations are often frustrated with the existing infrastructure. They might pressure the government to build bridges, dams, electrical plants, ports, and a phone system. All members of society will eventually benefit as the entire nation becomes wealthier. However, in the short run, while the nation is being developed, many of the poorest members may suffer and even die as funds that might otherwise be spent for humanitarian purposes are shifted to the building of infrastructure.

A way out of this predicament is to entice private capital from large foreign firms. This is often accomplished by offering large tax incentives or free land to foreign corporations. If foreign manufacturers can be encouraged to build facilities in poor countries that lack infrastructure, their money, along with the employment of local workers, will help lift a nation out of poverty.

Chapter 9:

The 4Ps And Web Marketing

Products and services are supplied by businesses for the benefit of businesses (business-to-business or B-to-B) or by businesses for the benefit of consumers (B-to-C). This distinction between the types of users of products and services has recently been redefined due to Web-based sales. "B-to-B" and "B-to-C" spaces are new terms to help express the rapidly changing distribution systems used by businesses. The word "space" as currently used defines a set of business activities generally related to specific markets. The Internet has allowed some typical B-to-B firms to market via the Web directly to the consumer bypassing well-established B-to-C firms. Some new Internet firms are selling B-to-C through a virtual retail store. Virtual Web stores bypass the very expensive process of building a real retail store (referred to as a "brick and mortar store"). This dramatic environment has shaken the very definition of the 4 Ps of marketing. We will follow the standard definitions but will also pose questions to better understand how marketing must adapt to the rapidly changing international and technology-driven environments.

Product

The product includes both products and services. The common perception is to think of products in a physical sense such as a car, a Coke, a massage, or having your palm read by a fortuneteller. Marketing professionals know a product defined by value added instead of physical features is very different. When you purchase your Coke are you:

a. After a cold drink?
b. Seeking a brand name you can rely on for consistent flavor?
c. Quenching a thirst?
d. Avoiding decisions about which brand is the best flavor?
e. Avoiding decisions about which brand is the best price?
f. Thinking about the last Coke commercial you saw?
g. Satisfied about the red color on the can (or bottle shape)?
h. Feeling as though you are part of a world order of youth that endorses Coke?
i. Feeling Coke is American and I like America?
j. Just wanting a Coke like the first Coke you had at the age of three and you don't even want to think about why you want it?

The list does not exhaust all the possibilities for the purchase of a Coke, a Pepsi, or any other soft drink for that matter. Similar lists can be made for most products and services. When you purchase the services of a fortuneteller are you:

a. After fun with your friends (entertainment)?

b. Buying a present for someone who would never purchase such a service on their own?

c. Really attempting to look ahead to the future?

Product design, color, image, taste, warranty, service availability, quality, consistency, repair facilities, financing, dependability, cost of repairs, texture, package, printed language instructions, web support, tech support, upgrades, and training are all important parts of the product. This list does not include the other 3Ps being the place, promotion, and price.

Manufacturers and service providers must analyze their potential markets prior to creating or altering products. The more buying motives you can satisfy with a product, the more total buyers you will have. How many buying motives can be satisfied with a certain product or service? Can more groups of people be served if the product is altered slightly? For example, can we alter Coke to become Coke Classic and gain new buyers? Perhaps, but can we do so without losing existing consumers who purchase for other motives?

(It is often very difficult for the maker of the product or provider of the service to fully understand why all their customers purchase their product. Many people ask the consumer why they purchased the product or if they were satisfied with the service provided. Leaving a small tip at a restaurant might indicate you liked the food but not the service or you liked the service but not the food. Cards placed on the table at some restaurants inquire about your level of satisfaction regarding both food and service. The card responses allow management to determine what part of your dining experience a customer liked and disliked. As a consumer, you will often find cards attached to product warranties that ask for personal information. The information collected from the card allows the company to gather a customer profile. The firm can then determine how to improve or alter the product to gain new customers without losing existing customers or how to sell you additional products and services).

Place -- Marketing and Distribution

Delivering the product or service at the right place and at the right time in good condition is a major component of a quality marketing program. Many products and services in today's marketplace will be transported many times, adding value at each stop, before the end consumer makes the purchase.

The product or service will move through what is called the distribution channel on its way to the end consumer. Buyers are other firms in the distribution channel adding value directly to the product or adding place value by locating the product where the final consumer can purchase it. Eventually, end users will purchase a product or service from the firm within a given distribution channel. Distribution channels are identified by the type of product. A person might talk about the distribution channel for bread, or flour, or wheat or food in general. Examples of an end user are:

1. A college student buying pasta and bread at a local grocery store where the retail grocery store is the final stop in the distribution channel for food.
2. A student purchasing a computer directly from a manufacturer's website is a modern Internet distribution channel, which concludes at the home where United Parcel or DHL delivers the product

Industrial customers use the product or service for their own business needs. Not all products find their way to retail stores (brick and mortar or virtual) and consumers.

Some products are designed and placed to satisfy businesses as the end user. Examples are:

1. A dump truck with snowplow attachment sold by Ford Motor Company to the local highway department
2. Six drums of hydraulic fluid sold to a firm that manufactures breakfast cereal
3. An accounting service for a local motel

Industrial buyers usually look for a good quality product, prompt delivery, and a competitive price. Because industrial buyers are less affected by emotions in their purchases than our retail customers, businesses in the supply chain focus on price, delivery, and good quality when promoting their products or services to industrial buyers rather than packaging or emotional appeal.

A firm selling cleaning supplies may promote its products by emphasizing the fact that it can deliver a wide assortment of goods within 24 hours. This will enable the buyer of these items to keep a minimum amount of supplies on hand, thus reducing the amount of money tied up in inventory. Just-in-time delivery of products and services allows firms to operate with less storage capacity and less money tied up in raw material inventories. It is critical in this type of operation to find businesses that can be depended on to deliver just-in-time.

Examine the marketing channel which exists between wheat growers to bread manufacturers presented in Exhibit 1. More channels are required to produce the product that we present in the exhibit. The exhibit only follows the wheat to bread channel with reference only to other supporting channels. The wheat to bread marketing channel requires numerous other channels in order to maintain the flow of product.

At some points in the channel, sales organizations arrange the sale between a seller and buyer without taking title to the goods. These brokers, agents, and sales representatives act just like a real estate agent would. They assist the buyer in arranging for the sale of a product. Each channel has a history that created the system through which the product moves. Some systems transfer title or ownership at each step. Other channels use agents or brokers to facilitate movement of the product.

In general terms, brokers work on large, one-time deals like a home sale. Agents generally represent the same client for many deals. Agents represent the buyer or the seller and on rare occasion represent both sides. An agent, for example, might represent the author of a spy novel and will continue to do so through many books and movie contracts.

A sales representative (sometimes called a manufacturer's representative) promotes the firm's product along with similar products from other firms. Sales reps (reps is the slang term used by most businesses) handle a wide variety of smaller transactions usually to retail store buyers.

Promotion

Retail Promotion:

- Your business must alert potential buyers that:
- Your product or service exists
- That you are ready to do business
- Provide directions to the location of the product (physical or Web).

Promotional activities must continue at some level as long as the firm is in business. Very few businesses secure a clientele and never have to be concerned about promotion thereafter. Perhaps small breakfast and lunch restaurants might be in the category of minimal promotion. But even these lucky businesses usually put out a lunch billboard or a list of specials at the point of purchase.

Wholesale/Distributor Promotion:

Assume you carry the right products from the right manufactures, have dependable delivery, extend credit, a state-of-the-art billing system, and a pleasant, hardworking and ethical staff. How can you market this image to firms? B-to-B firms must market their products and services both down the channel to the producer (manufacturer) and up the channel to other firms. To sell a firm down the marketing channel, you need to market your business as a valuable outlet for the manufacturer's products. Entering into the discussion to form a business relationship with a manufacturer, wholesaler or distributor will require the consideration of several items and attempted negotiation of:

- Extended terms on your invoices in order to delay payment
- The right to return poor quality merchandise directly to the manufacturer

- The exclusive right to sell the manufacturer's products in your territory
- Minimum order size (larger is better from the manufacturer's point of view)
- Turnaround time from order to delivery.

The results of negotiations establish the relationship and influences how wholesalers and distributors will relate to their clients.

Many business textbooks, when describing the flow of products in the marketing channel, show the arrows moving from producers to consumers. This describes the flow of physical goods, but not the flow of information and service. Wholesalers and distributors in the middle of the channel need to be concerned about promotion and service moving in both directions. That is, throughout the channel from retail store to the producer. Wholesalers and distributors need to inform producers and retail store buyers about the types of services they perform. They must also be prompt in meeting business obligations such as billing, paying bills, and responding to complaints. B-to-B relationships extend beyond the movement of product. The relationship provides a direct source of information about competitors and the response of customers to the product. The relationship also allows for discussions concerning price changes and technological changes in existing products.

Producer (Manufacturer):

Manufacturers are in the B-to-B market space except for a few attempting to reach the end consumer through the Web. Even though manufacturers sell to wholesalers and distributors in the B-to-B markets, it is essential that the firm seek answers to many questions about the end user.

- What do you need the buyers to know about your product or service?
- Do firms in the distribution channel and end consumers need instructions on how to use your product or service?
- Are the potential buyers aware that your product will satisfy a need that they have?
- Who will be using the product?
- Can potential buyers be identified by some characteristics? Do those characteristics fit any advertising vehicle that the firm can afford? For example, what advertising vehicle will hit the target market defined as teenagers 12 - 18 years old? What about the target market of working mothers?
- What strategies can be used to create demand for a new product or stimulate sales for an existing product?

In response to the last question, we next discuss two major strategies that can be used at all levels in the distribution channel but particularly at the manufacturing level.

The two strategies are the **push strategy** and the **pull strategy**.

The Push Strategy

We start the discussion by presenting a very common problem experienced by new producers. Assume indications are that consumers would purchase your product if it were available. To get the product to the consumer, the firm will need to move it through the distribution channel. Resistance will most likely be met all the way through that channel. Retail stores have only so many square feet of space to display products. While they do change their product mix to meet their customer's buying patterns, they prefer to stay with products, which are proven winners. Each square foot of space in a retail store is valuable. Retail store managers view each square foot of floor space as a rancher would view his orchard. Each tree in the orchard produces revenue just as each set of store shelves produce revenue. Both the tree and the square foot of retail space are capable of producing revenue. Both need the right mix of products and care at that exact spot. For a tree to produce good revenues they need the right mix of soil, pruning, fertilizer, pollination, pesticide, and harvesting. In the case of a retail store, the right mix to generate maximum revenues consists of location, parking, building design, interior shelves or stands, the buying and placing of products, pricing products, presentation, and finally the sale at the checkout point.

Every producer wants the prime space in the retail store -- the spot where every customer will look:

- Not too high
- Not too low
- Not in some remote spot in the retail shop.

Every time a product leaves the shelf and ends up at the cash register, the retailer brings home the money. Given products that have similar prices, the ones that sell fast (have a high turnover) will make the most money for a retailer.

Here then, is the manufacturer's problem. Why would a retailer give up profitable shelf space or square footage on the sales floor for an unknown, new product? This would be profitable right out of the retailer's pocket if the product sold slowly (had a low turnover rate), or worse yet, if the product did not sell at all.

The problem moves back through the distribution channel since the wholesaler will not carry a new firm's product unless the retailer is going to buy it. Wholesalers also have a shelf and floor space. They will only stock products with a high turnover, which is dependent on the retailer having a high turnover. How then, with such resistance existing in the marketing channels, can a new manufacturing firm push its products through the system? How can it encourage all levels in the distribution system to carry the product?

Advertising to both the wholesaler and retailer will help. Advertising in trade publications, such as magazines and newsletters that wholesalers and retailers in a particular line of business read, will inform the professional buyers of your existence. Price promotion to buyers within the channel will help get it started. Price promotion could be one free case with every twelve cases. It will take some study of the firm's unique distribution system to determine if the price discount should go to the wholesaler or the retailer. Maybe firms in the channel would prefer to have a price discount rather than a free product. It is important to discover what they would prefer, not what you as the producer would prefer.

Maybe instead of a price discount, a firm could offer free shipping. Or instead of shipping a pallet of product at a time, which would be preferable in the future, the manufacturer might agree to ship only a case at a time. For a new product, perhaps shipping in small quantities is preferred since there is less risk for everyone in the distribution system. This will increase some variable costs for the manufacturer, such as billing and transportation, but hopefully that will be a short run problem once the product has proven itself in the marketplace.

Another way to push a product is to provide sales training to other members in the channel. The manufacturer can explain how the product is made or used. This type of training is important in high priced goods such as furniture or technical products such as computers. It informs the other channel members about the distinctive product features and educates them on how to sell the product. This method of promotion can be very expensive.

In summary, a push strategy is aimed at informing members throughout the channel about the product and making it easier or more profitable to sell.

The Pull Strategy:

Now, imagine starting a business and despite your effort of making a quality product, pricing it strategically to penetrate the market, and promoting it throughout the marketing channel, you still cannot reach the break-even point (that is, make a profit). Not enough firms in the channel will handle your new product. If, after careful study, you are convinced the end consumer wants the product but the distribution system will not make room for it, you have three choices.

1. You can quit. Many firms do so at this point. If the firm was **undercapitalized**, that is, started without enough money, then there may not be any other choice. When plans are not fulfilled in a timely manner and money run out, then in hindsight, we can say the firm was undercapitalized. Running out of money might occur because the entrepreneur seriously underestimated the length required to penetrate existing markets. Funds are

needed to start the business. But once a business is started, it may take some time to earn the funds needed to keep the business working. The funds needed to keep the day-to-day operations of a business working are known as **working capital**. This is the money to keep people on the payroll, pay the electric bill, manufacture product, etc...

2. The second choice is to eliminate the middleman in the marketing channel. This takes an immense success drive and long-term stamina. This option is generally used only when the manager of the business is also the owner or at least one of the major stockholders. Self-preservation of ego will propel individuals to attempt great things.

3. The third option, if you cannot push your product or service fast enough through the marketing channels, is to go directly to the end consumer. Tell them about the product and encourage them to purchase it. This strategy is called the pull strategy. Final consumers will ask retail stores to carry the item. When retailers order, this "pulls" the product through the distribution channel. This method works very effectively, but it takes a lot of market research and a lot of money for promotional budgets.

Large firms that have been in business for some time can jump-start sales of a new product through the pull strategy. Rather than wait for the gradual development of the market, it might be faster (and more profitable in the long run) to both push and pull the product through the marketing channel. Large firms have the reputation and the money to get the attention of members of the distribution channel, to provide training or offer discounts. Large firms have the funding to send free samples via the mail system. They have the name recognition with final consumers to make advertising and promotion effectiveness, and they have money to afford advertising and promotion campaigns. They can run prime time ads and back up the national campaign with coupons in magazines and papers.

Even with such power in the marketing channels, however, many new products coming from large manufacturers still fail. Market research and test marketing can reduce the failure rate, but in the end, for the global corporation and for the small start-up venture, the product must fill a customer's need, it must be at the right place at the right time, it must be priced according to the value perceived by the customer, and it must be promoted in such a way that they know of its existence and desire it to fill a perceived need.

Business Communication and Advertising:

Businesses and organizations communicate in order to sell a product, belief, service, value or an image. They can do so in a one-way communication targeted toward a set of intended receivers. This is the advertising you see in magazines and on televisions. Businesses use many types of symbols to communicate the value of a product or service. Firms use logos, slogans, flags, and architecture to advertising. Most of us recognize some company symbols, such as the "golden arches" of McDonald's. For most of us, company symbols imply some particular level of quality, either high or low.

Businesses also use people as product symbols. These are the spokespersons that represent products. Jackie Joyner Kersey, a famous Olympic track star, for instance, was a spokesperson for Nike. Her athletic excellence is intended by Nike to transfer to its products. Of course, having a person as a product symbol can be risky. Dennis Rodman became famous as a basketball start playing for the Chicago Bulls. Rodman made some disparaging remarks about Mormons during the 1997 championship series. Not only did the NBA fine Rodman $50,000, but Carl's Jr., which had used Rodman in some of its television ads, yanked him permanently from further TV ads.

In marketing, "promotion" is comprised of five elements:

- Advertising
- Public relations
- Direct marketing
- Personal selling
- Sales promotion

Advertising is any paid form of non-personal communication through mass media.

Public relations is directed at building the image of the company and can be either paid or not paid. A common example of non-paid public relations is when a company gets a favorable story in a newspaper, magazine or TV. Larger companies have public relations departments that send press releases to media in the hopes of getting the stories aired or published. Companies will send new product information to an appropriate media channel, hoping that the channel will review the new product and present a favorable story.

Direct marketing is when a person (receiver) gets a message through a nonpersonal channel, such as mail, magazine, television, newspaper, or computer and orders the product by mail, phone, or computer.

Most of us, growing up as mall shoppers, are quite familiar with **personal selling**. For a marketer, personal selling is communication in a setting where the seller can anticipate questions or answer direct questions from the buyer. In personal selling, the seller and buyer are both sender and receiver. This is an interesting relationship, since, in some cases, the seller might not want to communicate certain information about the product, and might not "communicate" fully, or may falsely communicate.

It is the buyer's task to communicate questions clearly and precisely and to try to interpret the seller's messages accurately.

A sales promotion is any activity initiated for the short term to induce sales to any channel member or final consumer. Examples of sales promotion are coupons, rebates and price-off deals to final consumers. Quantity discounts to retailers or distributors are examples of sales promotions to channel members.

The five elements of promotion are often used together in an integrated marketing plan. Each element serves a specific purpose. Advertising creates product awareness, helps create sales, and builds a long-term image for a brand or company. Public relations help to build and maintain a positive company image over time. Sales promotion creates sales in the short run and helps build brand loyalty. Personal selling allows a company to provide different levels of information to buyers, and to answer product-related questions. The more complicated or technical the product, the more important personal selling becomes. Direct marketing allows marketers to reach buyers who may be difficult to reach in other ways or to reach them more cost-effectively.

Pricing

How does a business decide on a price to be charged for a product or service?

There are three choices to base price on:

- Cost
- Competition
- Demand

Price Based on Cost:

What price should a manufacturer, wholesaler or retailer put on a product? It is common sense that in most cases the price needs to be higher than what it cost the firm to make or buy the product. The difficult part of the common sense approach to pricing is to determine what the cost is.

When a product is manufactured it will have a labor cost and a raw material cost. Each time a unit of product is made, the total cost increases proportionately. Assume 15,000 units are made at a total labor and raw material cost of $900,000. To determine the per-unit cost, divide the labor and raw material cost of $900,000 by 15,000 (the number of units produced). The answer of $60 per unit is called the variable cost. The total cost varies directly with the number of units made. If no units are produced, variable costs are zero. If 15,000 units are produced, variable costs are $900,000 in total or $60 per unit.

Should you charge something more than $60? Yes, you need to cover other costs and make a profit. What if you offer your sales representatives $4.00 for each unit they sell? Add another $4.00 per unit to your variable cost. (Now variable cost is up to $64 per unit).

Unit Variable Costs	
Variable Costs	$60
Sales Rep. Commission	$4
Total Variable Costs	{$64}

To set the price, suppose the president of a company decides to mark the product up 25% over variable costs. The price of the product would be $80, or $16 above variable costs.

$$\$64 \times 25\% = \$16$$

$$\$16 + \$64 = \$80$$

The $16 difference between price and total variable costs per unit is called the contribution margin. This is the amount each unit "contributes" to pay other expenses such as fixed expenses (such as rent, salaries, and advertising) and profit if there is any after expenses.

Price Based On Competition:

Assume a marketing manager finds out that an established, competing firm is selling their units of a similar product for $76.

The President realizes that as a new company, they can't sell more products than their well-established competition, which has a good reputation and a cheaper price. Therefore, he/she may suggest lowering the unit price to $74. If a price is lowered, the unit contribution margin goes down. This leaves less money for covering expenses and squeezing out a profit. How many units must be sold so the company does not lose money? What we want to find is the point at which revenues from sales and costs (variable costs and fixed expenses) are equal. This point is called the break-even point. Selling additional units beyond this point will give us a profit.

We know that if we sell one unit at $74, we have a Contribution Margin of $10 to cover Fixed Expenses. This is summarized below:

Price	$74
Production Costs	$60
Sales Rep. Commission	$4
Less Total Variable Costs	$64
Contribution Margin	{$10}

To find out how many units a firm must sell to break even, divide the total fixed expenses by your contribution margin. The result will be the number of units you need to sell to break even:

Making a product or service that is somehow different from that of the competitors is called product differentiation. If successful in differentiating your product or service, pricing can then move away from that of the competitor. Product improvements and better quality standards are a good way to differentiate. However, sometimes advertising can build an image of a product being better differentiated than what actually exists.

The firm that has been able to differentiate its product has the option to not raise its price, but to keep the price near that of the competitor. The strategy in doing this is to gain more market share. Market share is the percentage of the market you service.

If Coca-Cola can make itself seem better or more desirable than Pepsi through advertising, do you think Coke would raise the price, or attempt to get more market share?

Price Based on Demand:

In our scenario, the firm has determined that $74.00 will "beat" the competition, resulting in the firm gaining some of the competitor's market share. Even at $74, the firm can produce a profit if 10,501 units or more are sold. The marketing manager needs to forecast demand for their industry and then estimate the firm's market share within that industry given the firm's price of $74.

The estimation process is in two stages. First, the firm must estimate demand for the entire industry. That is, how many people in a given market will want the product being sold by the industry? This is difficult to do, even with good historical data.

Hopefully, an industry association representing all the firms in that industry has been collecting data. In addition, financial firms such as banks, credit agencies, and stock market-related firms might have data.

Once industry demand has been forecast, the firm must estimate what its share of industry demand will be at a price of $74. How does price affect customer demand? If they charged $72.00 would the firm get a lot more market share? If they charged $75.00 would they lose many customers?

Demand is a function of many items. Demand is dependent on each of the 4P's. Is the product acceptable? Is it in the right place at the right time? Has it been well promoted? Is it priced right? Price is unique among the 4P's. It is the only variable that makes money. The other 3P's cost money.

Chapter 10:

Known And Unknown Ways To Grow Your Business Into A Million-Dollar Corporation

Building relationships

Take just 20 minutes of your time today and call 5 clients that purchased from you over the past week. The purpose of this call is to create a relationship only... with just 5 new clients. Do not try to sell them anything more at this point unless they bring it up. I only said to call 5, so don't call more than that or your business might increase too much. Please take the time to do it right now and see the amazing results! This is one simple action that can bring you more cash and more friends! Those are too things you just can't have too much of.

First introduce yourself and welcome them as a client. Even if you usually think of them as a customer, refer to them as a client from now on. I like the word client better because it makes people think of a long term relationship. Every single time you spend your valuable time, effort, and energy to acquire a business relationship you should consider it to be a long term relationship.

I have worked with clients that sell a onetime purchase product and I have always found ways of referring these clients to other companies which in return, they pay a referral fee. You must not under estimate the value of your network or database of client contacts. Next, begin to ask them about their purchase as an ice breaker. They will expect these types of questions since they just purchased from you. Make sure they are very happy with the total experience with your company from start to finish. Once you have built some rapport with them begin to ask about their personal life. Get to know them as a person.

Finish by letting them know you hope their experience with your company is always great and if you could do anything to make it better to please contact you personally. End by giving them your direct phone line and have them call you if they may ever need anything at all. Many times when I tell a client to do this they develop a bit of a twitch. Some business owners don't want to be contacted by their clients. I understand the hassle some clients can be but, don't underestimate their long term value.

Consider this, who in your company will handle a customer service issue once it gets too big and everyone else can't help solve it. YOU! Why not have a chance to solve a few of those issues when they are still small and easy to solve. Many times when a customer service issue gets to a business owner or CEO or top executive, the customer's biggest complaint is how long it's taken for them to get it resolved. Plus, when an issue is solved quickly, that customer can become your best client and refer more new clients.

Sell Yourself, Not Your Business

A successful business is one that is sold on who the owner or representative is, not the business itself. No matter what type of business you run, you are always selling yourself to the customer, not the business. You sell your expertise to customers, yourself to banks in order to receive funding and even sell yourself in order to gain marketing contacts and increase sales. You, essentially, are the face of your business. So when professionals say you need to "sell" in order to grow your business, they really mean sell yourself, not the idea of the company.

Trust is Key

Customers and business contacts need something to trust. A business name is not what they trust, they trust the person behind the business - you. What you say and do will greatly influence how customers and contacts view your business. Therefore, when you promise something, you better deliver it. Customers will put their trust into a business when you, the owner, put yourself out there and let your customers get to know you. By having a human being they can associate your company with, your company is much more likely to retain their business than those that simply sell their business "image" rather than themselves. Trust is an important tool for companies that want to increase sales and create wealth overall for the company.

Think About Where You Do Business

Think about another small business that you do business with. Most likely you work with that company because a sales representative, the owner or another key staff member made an impression on you in some way to make you relate, trust and want to work with that company. The company didn't just jump the gun and want to sell you're their products; they sold you on themselves first. If you use the same approach as companies you currently associate with and add that "personal" level into your marketing, you will improve profit and be able to grow your business simply on selling you, not your company.

Create a Connection

The bottom line is a customer wants to learn about you before they learn about what you are selling. Take the extra time to get to know your customer, find out their needs, but not with the goal of a sale in mind. By creating a real, genuine connection with your customer you have the ability to increase sales. Why? Because people don't deal with strangers, they deal and do business with those they know.

The Bottom Line

Customers and contacts come back to the businesses they like and to like a business, they have to have a person to associate with it. By creating an effective sales technique that integrates that personal touch, you can create wealth from simply being yourself.

Mastermind Groups

Mastermind groups are a great way to get new ideas, stay connected and grow your business. Napoleon Hill introduced the idea of mastermind groups in his book, Think and Grow Rich which was first published in the 1930s. While the name, Mastermind, suggests extraordinary intelligence, the idea is really very simple and very powerful and allows for almost anyone to be part of a Mastermind group.

A Mastermind Group is really nothing more than a group of people with a common purpose that meet on a regular basis to share ideas, discuss challenges and encourage each other. However, the way in which the group operates is really only limited by the groups creativity. As long as the group is an agreement, anything is possible.

Before starting or joining a Mastermind Group, make sure you are ready. There are billions of networking and business groups in the world that rarely accomplish anything because the people involved lack the focus and drive to make them work. No matter what a group is called or how it is designed to operate, the people that make up the group will ultimately decide how effective and productive it is.

5 things to consider before joining a Mastermind Group:

1. **Participate.** If you are not willing to actively participate in the group by sharing your ideas, challenges and encouragement, then don't join the group. I personally have been in a number of groups where we may have ten people in the group but 99% of the conversation came from 3 or 4 people. A Mastermind Group is different, all members must contribute. If you don't think you can, don't join.

2. **Trust is a key element of a Mastermind Group.** The members of the group have to be able to be able to trust that the details discussed in the meeting will stay with the members of the group. Violating this trust will end the group and probably the your relationship with the members of the group.

3. **How big will your group be?** I expect the average size is 6 - 8 people but I also know that there are groups with much higher member counts. Obviously if you are joining an existing group this may already be decided but you still need to be comfortable with the size of the group. If you are starting a group, be sure to identify how you want the group to operate and size it accordingly.

4. **How often will you meet?** While this will probably be one of the Group's first decisions, not just yours, you need to know what you are comfortable with. I personally like groups that meet weekly. Many people hear weekly and immediately say that they are too busy and don't have the time. Well, here's the thing, this Group is supposed to add

value to your business, not just be another thing that sucks up your time. If it adds value then you can't afford not to do it.

5. **Invitation only.** Remember this group is going to be productive and is going to help your grow your business so you must be picky about how is in it. You cannot allow someone in the group just to be nice because chances are that person will only take from the group if not end up being a distraction. For the Mastermind Group to really be effective, it must be focused and controlled. Unfortunately in today's world is seems difficult to exclude people but that is exactly what you have to do if you want your group to succeed.

Mastermind Groups can be very powerful if they are designed and controlled correctly. Humans weren't created to go at things alone, we need companionship and help. A Mastermind Group can bring together groups of people that have similar needs and build a community where you don't have to figure everything out on your own. Join or start a Mastermind Group today and prepare to grow your business.

Prosperity Partnering

Joint ventures and strategic partnering are common marketing strategies. Many entrepreneurs have extended their reach, impact, and profits by joining with others to reap the benefits of business synergy. Prosperity Partners are above and beyond the

JV mindset; it's about finding people you connect with at a deeper level and allowing that connection to be the foundation of a shared prosperity goal.

Finding a Prosperity Partner may be easier than you think. First you have to be in the stream of life rather than sitting on the bank watching the beautiful sailboats go by. Too often people won't jump in because they are waiting for all their ducks to line up - they never do; they are waiting for life to slow down - it never does; they are waiting for the approval or cooperation of others - which isn't likely to come any time soon.

If you have a list of reasons why you are not going for your passion or playing full-out, you may be feeling uninspired or burdened by your own dreams to be, to do, to have. Prosperity Partnering is a powerful tool for keeping yourself enthused and on track. The only thing required to attract powerful and amazing Prosperity Partners is you showing up in your own life as powerful and amazing ... which you are. Trust me on that one. You are brilliant, resourceful, creative, and you can bring all that forward right now. If you mistakenly believe that you can't get started until you have all the answers and you have to know all the ins and outs before you can embrace your passion, I invite you to change the belief right now. Another deterrent could be if you are addicted to self-improvement and you are stuck in a cycle of learning one more thing before you feel confident in what you already know.

There could be many reasons why you are not moving forward with confidence. Use this EFT Choices (TM) Style Affirmation to help release you from this psychological form of bondage; Even though I don't have all the answers right now, I choose to move forward with confidence and ease. When you stop stopping yourself, selling yourself short, you will begin to attract people who see your inner brilliance and respect you for it. Your gifts and talents are so second nature to you and they may seem so ordinary to you that you take them for granted. Someone on the outside, a potential Prosperity Partner, may see these very qualities as star qualities that would be a great compliment to their own strengths.

As you move forward, you will observe that there are people who naturally resonate with you and others who do not. You will become skilled at forming new positive relationships and support networks and from those connections you can set an intention to attract your team of Prosperity Partners. A Prosperity Partnership is not a legal contractual agreement, it's a soul agreement. It carries more weight that the human law can enforce because this kind of partnership is consciously leveraging **Universal Laws**. Prosperity Partners understand the implications of the Law of Attraction in how they conduct their personal lives and their business. Integrity and ethics are part of their core and this is not to say you should not sign legal contracts to guide your business interactions, it's just a reminder that a contract won't assure you that you are in a Prosperity Partnership.

It may take you a few misses before you get it right. That certainly was my experience. I think the shift came for me when I realized I could be successful without depending on others and that's when I was able to attract Prosperity Partners who were operating from an equal position. Co-dependency is not a basis for any viable partnership and it certainly has no place in a Prosperity Partnership. It's about interdependence and synergy at its best; like a great marriage. Prosperity Partners won't have the same strengths or weaknesses, but they will have strengths and unique perspectives that are perfect to compliment one another. They add value to each others offering and they support and encourage personal success outside of the business context. This is a very powerful relationship. If you want a Prosperity Partner, step into the stream, ignite your passion and set an intention to attract the perfect Prosperity Partners with confidence and ease.

Collaborate on Goals and Plans

The process for growing your individual talent begins when you or your managers engage in discussion with direct reports to understand each employee's personal and professional goals and how these goals align with the current and future needs of the business. Working with managers to establish goals and development plans, the employee takes ownership of his personal development. Managers coach, provide feedback, and offer opportunities for learning experiences and new challenges that push growth.

Managers can learn a lot by talking with employees about what interests them. As business goals are defined and roles and responsibilities are clarified, it is up to managers to ensure that individuals have the opportunities to develop their knowledge and skills in areas that interest them. This is part of their collaboration. It is of mutual value to the individual and the company because people who are doing what they enjoy and what is exciting to them are more productive. One company needed to solidify its brand. No one on staff had expertise in branding, but an employee had expressed an interest in learning and developing in this area. With her manager, she identified excellent training programs. She worked closely with a consultant hired by the company to work with her on the rebranding efforts, which were successful for the company and made the employee even more dedicated to the company because she was given the opportunity to grow.

Freedom and Accountability

Delegating is often a big stretch. But it is easier to let go and give others responsibilities when you provide boundaries for authority and decision-making. We call this "the area of freedom." Imagine a sandbox framed on each side by these parameters:

- Values that are core to your culture
- Policies and procedures for your company
- Job descriptions and standards of performance objectives that describe what the work is and what must be accomplished
- Business goals

Defining these boundaries makes it clear to employees where they can operate with a degree of freedom. To respect this freedom, you and other leaders/managers need to maintain a respectful distance along with appropriate dialogue and feedback.

Here's an example of how it works. Clients ask the sales manager of a tech company for a quote on integrating two technologies. His team has extensive experience with both technologies and wants to offer a different solution. They already know that these technologies do not work well together. The clients aren't open to listening to an alternative solution. They keep pushing the sales manager for a quote on integrating the two technologies, which he knows will only mean problems for them. He could give them a quote, and his company could do the work, but he knows it's not right. The clients will not be happy with the final solution. He would meet his goal, but the longer-term cost to the company would be too high. Knowing that each project reflects the company's values and he is responsible for reflecting the value of excellence, the sales manager chooses to explain to the clients the reasons why his firm has decided not to offer a quote on the project. Frustrated and disappointed at first, the clients eventually understood the problematic nature of the technology and they asked the sales manager to propose another solution.

Without the "sandbox," the sales manager could have proposed a quote for the job. The firm could have done the work, charged the clients, and the clients would have gotten what they requested. The sales manager would have met his goals for the year and probably received compensation for doing so. However, this would have happened at great cost to the company and its reputation; it would have been a shortsighted decision.

Push Down and Spread Out Decision-Making

The people on the front lines need to have the freedom and accountability to make good decisions. They are in a position to notice things, small things that can make big differences. Often good ideas are suppressed or wasted because people don't feel empowered to bring them to anyone's attention, or take initiative to develop them.

When I worked as a purchasing manager at a big packaged-food company, a veteran maintenance supervisor, Ernie had figured out a way to save a lot of money. He quietly began substituting nylon rollers for steel rollers on the track that moved products along the production line. Ernie worked under the radar, because this improvement meant breaking regulations requiring stainless steel rollers. But the nylon rollers lasted ten times longer and reduced wear on supporting parts. Ernie's quiet innovation was saving the company $60,000 per machine per year, but he was afraid to ask for management approval. I persuaded a government inspector to OK the change, reported the savings to management and when the company picked up on the idea, other plants adopted it. The company saved $1 million a year thanks to Ernie, a guy who knew the production equipment better than anybody else but had no voice in the company.

The front lines are where good ideas need to flourish and decisions need to be made. Smart business owners train and empower everyone to make decisions that serve the company's strategy by providing some guidelines and frameworks, like the "sandbox," to encourage innovation and leadership at all levels. People need to feel that they have the freedom and authority to speak up, to solve problems and pursue ideas. Leadership can come from anyone anywhere.

The implications of spreading freedom and accountability through your organization can be transformative. Wes, owner of an IT firm, took a long-needed two-week vacation with his family. When he returned, he expected to find a stack of work that would take days to dig through. Instead, he found little and was finished in a day and a half. When he realized he didn't have anything to do, that his desk was clean, he had a sense of sheer terror. Before implementing professional management, that kind of lapse in activity for him would have meant his business was in crisis. If he didn't have anything to do, that meant his company didn't have anything to do. He realized it was a signal that everything was going exactly as designed. His managers and other employees were well prepared to assume more responsibility and make decisions. His desk was clean because his employees were doing what they were supposed to do.

Hold People Accountable

A common complaint from business owners is that their employees are not accountable for their work. Or they believe that their employees don't work hard enough, put out enough effort to help the business to be successful. When we ask business owners, "How much more is enough? What exactly do you want from them?" they can't answer those questions clearly. Instead of negotiating goals and clarifying expectations, business owners assume that their employees already know what is expected. This is a big mistake, an incorrect assumption, and it creates a gap or misunderstanding in your relationship with your employees. It doesn't serve you, your business, or your employees.

To motivate employees to work hard and help the company to succeed, you need to talk with them. Discuss your expectations and listen to theirs. Try to bring both into alignment so that everyone has a mutual understanding and a satisfactory relationship. I've found that most employees want to contribute and to be successful; they just need direction and clear communication on what is expected. Many genuinely want to exceed expectations, but they can do so only if they know what those expectations are.

Chapter 11:

Effective Use Social Media For Incredible Expansion & Growth

What is Social Media?

Social media is a category of online media where people are talking, participating, sharing, networking, and bookmarking online. Examples include Facebook, Twitter, LinkedIn, YouTube, GooglePlus, and MySpace.

What is Social Media Marketing?

Social media marketing is using the above-mentioned platforms to reach a new audience of consumers and create product brand awareness. By spreading word of a product from user to user, Social Media Marketing strives to gain greater legitimacy for a message because it is shared between trusted "friends."

Which Social Media Channels are most popular?

Studies show that Facebook & Twitter are most popular social media channels followed closely by YouTube and LinkedIn, GooglePlus.

Why should Social Media Marketing Interest me?

If you think this kind of Marketing is not for you, think again. These platforms offer a large bundle of benefits to small business owners. Here are some reasons why you should consider using Social Media for your business.

Exposure: As a small business owner you rely largely on network marketing to channel leads to your business - which, in turn, relies on your interaction with people. This is the core notion of what Social Media is! But Social Media offers virtually unlimited opportunities to interact with people - millions of them! With this interesting form of marketing, your business is no longer limited to local leads; you will find leads coming in from a diversified geographic market!

Zero - cost: While other marketing media would be expensive, this type of marketing is relatively free, or requires negligible monetary investment. It's a great low-cost way to get your message across.

Improved web presence: Being on popular social media platforms strengthens your web presence. The more people talk about you on Facebook or Twitter, the greater are the chances of your business being found on relevant web searches such as Google, Yahoo!, or Bing.

Direct contact with prospects: These platforms put you in touch with your customers directly. You can have one-on-one contact with them, know what they really want.

Go viral: Such marketing offers you the opportunity to go viral with your marketing. Think about this. You put up a video about your business on YouTube. 10 people like it, and five of them share it with their friends, who in-turn share it with 20 more people. This is known as "viral marketing," and it can be a very effective method to increase your lead generation.

What is a Social Media "game plan" and why should you have one?

A social media game plan is a process consisting of a few simple steps that can help you achieve your social media marketing objectives. The social media arena is large and you can get lost in it if you don't play by the rules. There's a lot of competition and you have to have a clear plan if you want to stand out of the crowd and get noticed.

Your ideal Social Media game plan

A typical game plan for your business should consist of these four steps

1. Build your network
2. Propagate your presence

3. Stay connected

4. Monitor

Step 1 - build your network: The first step is to search for and add those users to your network whom you think fall into your target audience segment. When placing a request to add users to your network, it is always better to accompany such requests with a personalized message. You can also look for and join groups that pertain to your line of business. For example, if you are a business selling Health drinks and other health-related products, you could join groups where topics such as nutrition, diet or health are discussed. Such groups provide you audience for the products you have to offer. However, when in a group, do remember to ADD VALUE. Answer questions that you are equipped to answer, actively participate in discussions, be subtle and don't aggressively "push" your products.

Step 2-propagate: The next step is to announce your Social Media presence. You can do this by adding links to your social media pages on your website, e-mail signature line or newsletter, if you have one. You are out there with your business-announce it!

Step 3-stay connected: The third step is to stay connected with your fans and group members. Social media marketing initiative is easy to start, but requires effort to maintain. And like many networking efforts, results are usually not immediate. Acquire permission from group members and others on your network to send e-mails. You can then e-mail relevant content to people on your network. The key here is to send RELEVANT, VALUE ADDING content-not an advertisement of your products/services. If you are a health-drink selling company who is also a part of the diet and nutrition group, you can send links such as '10 Best Anti-Oxidant Rich Fruits' and then perhaps add an image and some information about your product, encouraging people to get in touch with you if they're interested. This approach will be better-received than just sending the prospects an e-mail flyer totally dedicated to your product.

Dos and Don'ts

While social networking is all about human interaction and cannot be strait-jacketed, here are some tips that will come in handy.

What you should do?

Add value to your contacts: Always add value to your contacts. Always! Provide them useful information, tips and other interesting facts that they can use. For example, Jane, a home-based business owner sells health drinks and weight loss products. So, it makes sense for her to provide her audience with interesting articles on the topic of weight loss.

Be consistent in your online participation: It is not a one-time effort. It is about building a relationship... and relationships take time. Be consistent in your social media communication. Have an interesting tweet/post/update at least every day. In some few cases, multiple postings a day are even better-but don't forget rule#1-add value. Your posts shouldn't sound like pointless ramblings or advertisements of your product/service.

Pay attention to what's being discussed: If you have joined a forum or a group, actively participate in relevant discussions. Use your specific, professional knowledge to help others. Contribute to add depth and dimension to a discussion.

Conversation is the key: As mentioned before, social media marketing thrives on relationships. To build a strong relationship with your prospects, you need to engage in a conversation with them. Maintain a 2-way communication between you and your audience. Take genuine interest in what they have to say and follow up on comments or observations that are made.

Thoroughly know the subject you are talking about: Position yourself as an expert on these platforms. But be sure that you know what you're talking about. Research if you aren't sure of something. Mistakes on these platforms spread quickly and damage the reputation of your business.

Personalize your interaction: It's advisable to personalize your interaction with your audience. Inquire about an event or occasion posted on a Wall, such as a recent trip, or "like" their vacation pictures on Facebook.

Portray your individuality: The biggest advantage small business owners have over large corporations is the fact that they are much smaller and haven't lost that real-person feel. Let your audience know the person behind the business. Make sure your interactions include a personal side!

Respond to your customers' grievances ASAP: Did you know that 88% of customers say unanswered complaints on social media sites deter them from doing repeat business? And deleting customer complaints is even worse! So make sure you resolve your customer's complaints on social media platforms immediately. Even if you can't resolve them, at least respond so that they know they're being heard. Acknowledge everything.

Mention your Social Media presence: Advertise your profiles. Always provide links to your social media profile in your website, blog, e-mails and even print materials. For websites and blogs, it's best to add Facebook and twitter widgets which provide a live feed of what's happening on your Facebook/twitter page, right there on your website or blog. Provide incentives or value adding information such as whitepapers or articles in order to encourage people to follow you on social media sites!

Monitor & moderate: Monitor your social media presence. Find out where your name's coming up online and in what context it has been used. A Google alert is the simplest way to do this, though there are many free tools available online to monitor your web presence. Also stay in-control of your social media pages. Read what others are putting up on your page and respond promptly.

Syndicate your Social Media content: Content creation takes time. So why not make the most of the content you have? Post your content on all popular social media sites and don't hesitate to re-use them. Turn a blog post into a link and put it on Facebook. Convert it into a video and add to YouTube and Facebook or turn it into a presentation and put it up on SlideShare. The aim is to get maximum exposure for your content.

What you should not do?

DON'T overtly push your products/services: Social media is a platform where you build relationships, to create value. It's NOT an advertising venue. Your audience will shun you if all you talk about is the stuff you sell. Think about it, would you talk to your family and friends about the products you sell all the time? Of course not! Then don't treat your social media audience any differently.

DON'T spam your contacts with pointless updates: OK, so now you added two new products to your line-up. While it's great to share the news, don't spam your contacts with ads. Put up a link to the new range of products; monitor who is interested and share information on a need-to-know basis.

DON'T have grammar and spelling errors in your posts: You are a small business out to create an impression. Don't spoil it through spelling and grammatical errors. Use spelling/grammar checking tools if possible, but never rely solely on them. Proofread your posts before putting them up online. If spelling or grammar is not your strong suit, have someone else proofread your work before it goes out.

DON'T fail to respond to requests for help in your area of expertise: If you are a part of a group or forum, seize every opportunity to display your expertise. Don't be a wallflower-actively participate in discussions.

DON'T let your profile get stale: Make sure your profile is frequently updated and that you offer something new. One mistake many small business owners make is creating social media profiles and then forgetting about them. Your social media efforts have to be on-going to bear results.

DON'T get distracted: There's a lot of distraction available online-especially on social media channels that can make you lose track of your productive hours online. Games, quizzes, forums and live-chats-while these can be interesting tools to attract prospect interest, focus on your goals. Otherwise, you'll find yourself investing too much time and energy into activities that offer no returns to your business.

Chapter 12:

Six Critical Game-Changing Business Habits

Let me tell you straight, you cannot be a successful business person if you don't have good business habits. Below I have listed a few habits that you should be doing if you wanted to be a successful business person.

1) Are you committed to every business you have?

Opening a business is easy but maintaining its operation will take a lot of you time. Will you be available in creating marketing plans and promotional materials? Business without marketing plans is suicide. Once you start a business, put every attention to it. Don't let your employees manage it. Take note of this, you are the only person who has vision for its success so its only you who can make it grow.

2) Are you continuously searching for opportunities?

Business people don't just stick on 1 or 2 business. A business person always searches for more business opportunities. They are not mediocre. They don't want stable business but rather a growing one. Always search for new ideas to pursue. A business person has a vision for numerous income streams for profits!

3) Do you think positively of your business?

A business person don't pursue a business to which he/she doesn't feel positive about. Once you start a business, don't fill your mind with any negative thoughts. Problems may come your way but it will always have a solution. Business people don't think of failures, always success behind every problem.

4) Do you share the business vision?

You can't survive on your own. You may be skillful at some point but it can't make you very successful. A business person shares a business vision, to someone else, to a possible business partner. If a single business person can earn $1000 a month, then 2 person can earn $2000 a month. Simple logic but its reality. You can earn more as long as you share same vision with someone else.

5) Do you delegate tasks?

Normally, every business person only thinks of opportunities and its corresponding marketing campaigns. It will not be healthy if the business person will also do the action of implementation. He will be a dead meat if he/she will put every burden unto their shoulders. In fact, employees purpose is to put every plan into action, right?

6) Do you create a good public image?

People are very sympathetic. They support the business whom they like the owner. Whether you like it or not, if people like your attitude and way of doing business, they will support you. But if you look like a bad boy or a person who looks down and criticizes people, believe me, you will loose every customer you've got!

Start creating a good public image. Help support the community where you belong. Extend some help to those in need. Don't act as if what's the only thing important to you is your profits and earnings. Make the public see that you care.

Chapter 13:

Why Do People Fail In Business & How Can You Avoid Total Failure?

It is a sad fact that every day businesses fail.

In fact, to be more accurate, in a normal year on average around 50 companies go into liquidation on every business day of the year. During a recession such as in 1992 that figure went up to over 90. And that's just the companies. It doesn't include the sole traders and partnerships that go under as well.

So why do businesses fail?

Business failures are a bit like fires. Something smoldering may be difficult to see but can be relatively easy to put out with little damage or risk if caught early. Once a fire is really going, it is much easier to see, but is usually much more difficult and dangerous to extinguish as it consumes resources, and crucially, cash.

Cash is king as the old saying has it. And no one believes this more deeply than turnaround executives. Because fundamentally businesses fail when they run out of cash.

And while there are well established ways of tackling businesses that are starting to burn their cash, one of the major problems for turnaround professionals is that we are often called in too late.

You would call the fire brigade if you saw a burning house. If you see a business that is fire fighting, it is time to call in the business fire brigade, a company doctor.

What causes business failure?

There are really four types of business failure.

Firstly there is the start up that never does. It's a well known statistic that most businesses cease trading within their first three years. In many ways this is an inevitable result of the willingness of entrepreneurs to take the risk of starting up and testing the market.

Given how difficult it can be to raise money for a new venture, many such businesses have so few resources to start out with that a relatively small set back in the early years can be sufficient to wipe them out, where a larger business would pull through. Having got through these critical first three years however, business failures then fall into three main camps.

Catastrophic business failures where the business suddenly 'falls off a cliff' are the second type of failure. While often being high profile, these are actually quite rare and are often due to the impact of some traumatic event such as a major fraud, lost litigation or sudden change in the law.

The third type of failure, overtrading, by contrast is a relatively common cause of business failure in boom times as businesses grow faster than their cash resources can support.

But most failures are of the fourth type and follow what has come to be known as the business decline curve where a business that is underperforming, starts to become distressed and as the decline steepens, falls into crisis and eventual failure.

How do you spot the warning signs?

One particularly frightening thing about the decline curve is how as a business descends the slippery slope, problems start to compound.

An underperforming business makes lower levels of profit than its competitors. With less profits it can reinvest less into the business. Slowly, insidiously, it starts to slip behind and over time market reputation and share are lost, resulting eventually in the first losses being recorded.

As it has to fund losses, a business in distress starts to stretch and juggle its cash. The bank manager wants security and personal guarantees as the account starts to be constantly up against the overdraft limit, and the business starts to delay sending in management accounts; the business starts to stretch payments to suppliers and subcontractors or make round sum payments on account as a way of eking out the available cash. The staff know that the business has problems and morale and quality of work sinks.

By the time it is in a crisis the finance director has either jumped ship or has gone off on long term sick leave. It is on stop with its suppliers and the CCJs are starting to fly. So sub-contractors are stopping work and the business cannot get the materials needed to complete its contracts or products and so collect in cash from its customers.

And if it cannot get the cash in to pay the rent or the wages at the end of the month, suddenly it's all over.

What causes normal business failure?

So how do businesses get themselves into these sorts of situations?

There seem to be five main contributing factors to most 'normal' business failures in varying degrees.

Firstly and usually most importantly, there are management problems. The autocratic managing director whose drive has been vital in the past, but is now driving the business into the ground while simultaneously driving away anyone who tries to disagree; the board dispute that has led to civil war; the lack of anyone who really understands what the numbers are telling them; the family company run in the interests of family members and not the business's needs. Any and all of these sorts of issues can prevent the business recognising or dealing with the problems facing it.

Because secondly, any business needs to have an eye out for the strategy challenges that it will inevitably face, whether these are changes in the market and customers demands; technological changes that require reinvesting and moving on; or changes in the competition which require improved efficiencies to keep the cost base competitive.

The third area is a lack of financial control, where it is usual to find that cash has become tied up in old stock, debt or retentions; that lack of proper reporting means costs are actually out of control (is all that machinery we are paying hire charges for really still on site?), management do not have accurate costings so they do not really know how much margin each job is making, and there is weak control of variations and valuations so the eventual outcome is uncertain.

Fourthly there is a lack of operational control of both hard issues such as up to date machinery and the soft issues of organizational structure and staff management.

Finally there are any 'big project' such as a new computer system, a problem acquisition, a huge new contract, or a premises move. Anything that adds extra disruption to the business, while taking away cash and management time can prove to be the straw that breaks the camel's back.

Chapter 14:

7 Proven Ways To Turn Past Failures Into Success

Perhaps your professional life isn't going exactly like you thought it was supposed to go. Maybe you've made a series of bad decisions or even one really bad choice that you can't seem to bounce back from. Maybe you've been downsized or terminated. Maybe your best-laid plans have failed and circumstances beyond your control--from market downturns to bad weather to a key player's incompetence--have put you in the danger zone, or even out in the street.

You may not realize it right now, but you do have options. You could wallow in self-pity, or remain angry at those whom you blame for your current situation. Or you can turn your past disappointments into great accomplishments. How? Just follow the path of the heroes who've gone before you. They will show you how to transform past adversity and failures into springboards for success.

Tip No. 1: Take An Objective, Not an Emotional Look, At Where You've Come From

Thomas Edison believed there were no such things as mistakes, only eliminated options that brought him one step closer to his goal. There is no such thing as "failure," he claimed, only lessons to be learned.

Most people find it difficult to see a failure in an analytical, impartial fashion; many of us were raised to believe that if we failed at something, we were failures. Therefore, as adults, we take failure personally, believing our lack of success indicates a lack in our character. Instead, we must look at the situation objectively, as a matter of cause and effect. The fact that we fail in business situations does not mean we are failures, but rather that we didn't create the right cause to achieve the desired effect.

If you find yourself in a stuck emotional state, go back and analyze the steps you took and see what you might have done differently. Remove the emotional involvement; just look at the raw data. Logically and dispassionately examine the course you chose and determine why it did not yield the result you wanted, and then consider why it was not appropriate for that particular situation. You'll need to acknowledge what you did that led to the failure, and take responsibility for it. But, like Thomas Edison, you should take what you can learn from it and move on.

Tip No. 2: Focus on the purpose on the other side of the pain.

Happiness does not come from the elimination of pain, but from the realization of your purpose. Keep reminding yourself why you are doing what you're doing. Even less lofty purposes, such as "I just work here to pay the rent and my car payment," can be transformed over time if you look at the higher purpose for why you might be there. Perhaps you will make contacts that will help you in the future. Perhaps you are trying to save money to put your kids through college. The key is to look beneath the surface to find the spiritual meaning.

To succeed, you'll need to look at the higher goals you've set and determine their importance, then focus on what is good, important, and meaningful to you, rather than on the mundane aspects or the things you hate about your job. If you develop a strong enough reason or purpose to keep going, and you can focus on that purpose, you will succeed at each of the steps you take toward your goal. Without a sense of purpose, you will lack motivation and consciously or subconsciously doom yourself to failure.

Tip No. 3: You can't see the whole parade from where you stand.

You never know from where you stand whether what you are experiencing will turn out to be good or bad until enough time has passed. A seemingly hopeless situation may be exactly the disaster you fear, but it may also turn from catastrophe into triumph in ways you are unable to predict.

When people get stuck in "Why me?" mode as a result of a severe business loss, they require a mindshift in order to recover a sense of belief, hope, and inner strength so they can move on. If we can look outside of ourselves at others who have overcome adverse circumstances, we can gain the courage to believe in our ultimate success. In your industry, who do you know or have heard of who failed but managed to get back on top, perhaps in another industry altogether? History is filled with examples.

Soichiro Honda persevered through countless failures and setbacks, over four decades, before his Honda Motor Company became one of the largest automobile companies in the world. His inspiring story demonstrates the power of perseverance in the face of adversity and the necessity of innovation and creativity in periods of failure and loss.

When we make a deliberate decision not to give up, then life seems to present opportunities we had not thought of or could not create ourselves.

Tip no 4: It's not whether you have won or lost in the past; it's the person you have to become in order to win in the future.

After a business failure has led you to analyze the objective data of your experience, you then need to look at the kind of person you need to become to see the results you want in the future. Beyond visualizing the physical objects or the status you seek, you need to look within and say, "What kind of person do I need to become in order to get what I want?"

To become that person, you may need additional education or training in your field or another career; you may need to hire a coach or find a mentor to guide you through the steps to becoming who you want to be. Or you may require a character shift, to be reborn, in a sense. Lance Armstrong, for example, had never won a single Tour de France before he was diagnosed with testicular cancer. Then it looked like his cycling career, and maybe even his life, were over. He fought back hard and won. Today he credits his great cycling success to the person he became as a result of having cancer. He says, "Cancer saved my life."

Tip No. 5: Accept that falling is a normal part of life, but try to fall forward every time--in the direction of your goal.

We are all continually creating our own destinies through the choices we make and our desire and determination to see them through. Perhaps you've suffered a major business defeat such as downsizing or termination. Realize that you can leave that job on good terms with a handshake and a letter of recommendation, or with the threat of a lawsuit against those who fired you. How you handle the crisis has a dramatic impact on how you will succeed from that point forward.

For example, early in his football coaching career, Lou Holtz was fired from his job at the University of Arkansas for no apparent reason. He could have sued, sulked or slandered. But instead, he shook hands and moved on, keeping the good friends he had there. From there, he went to the University of Minnesota. When his dream job at the University of Notre Dame job came open, Holtz' applied. Notre Dame started calling Holtz' past employers - including the University of Arkansas. Arkansas gave him a raving recommendation and Notre Dame hired him. Holtz finally got his dream job where he won several national championships. Had Holtz chosen to react negatively after being fired at Arkansas, he would have virtually guaranteed a bad performance review, which could have cost him his dream job at Notre Dame. How we react to bad things today has a huge impact on what happens to us tomorrow.

Like Lou Holtz, you can choose to fall in the direction of your next goal, deciding to treat the fall as a sort of awkward but valuable step along the path of your life and career. If instead of dwelling on the circumstances of the past, you can manage to move on in a forward direction, your fall will send you in the direction of your goals.

Tip No. 6: "Retreat" does not equal "defeat."

A retreat can be a valuable opportunity to regroup and rethink strategies and goals. For example, one of the worst business mistakes you can make is to continue to pour money into a failing business; in this situation, knowing when to call it quits and creatively develop a better plan is essential.

Don't let pride keep you stuck in a wrong decision. Managers and investors need to be willing to change a course of action that isn't working, no matter how much faith, time, and money may have been put into it so far. You need to be willing to abandon a path that is not taking you where you want to go and start over again.

Captain Oliver Hazard Perry is famous for captaining the ship that bore the flag saying "Don't give up the ship" during the War of 1812. The little known fact is that he did abandon that ship! When 80% of his men were dead and his ship was sinking, he paddled a little john-boat over to another ship, took control of it, and soundly defeated the British in the Battle of Lake Erie.

Tip No. 7: Realize that pain and heartache are only labor pains before your birth.

Many people who lost their jobs and businesses as the economy took a downturn have searched for years and have yet to find a job in their industry. This loss may have a profound effect on their sense of self. Like Moses after he was stripped of his wealth and power and was exiled into the desert by Pharaoh, they may feel as if all is lost, as they find themselves doing work they never would have envisioned themselves doing when they were in college. But Moses' many years of exile in the desert was exactly what he needed in order to become the kind of man who would eventually free the Hebrews from slavery.

In any painful, frightening situation, you need to realize that there is hope on the other side of the tragedy, even if you can't see it yet. When you quit, you guarantee that you will not be around to experience that which makes your suffering count for something. Turn your pain into a purpose.

If you persevere, you will gain wisdom and perspective and finally realize why you went through everything: namely, to become a new person, the person you needed to become in order to achieve the success you were seeking.

Claim Your Future Success

Many heroes of the past have blazed a trail for us to follow if we really want to overcome tragedies and failures. Remember, just because you may have failed does not mean you are a "failure." Failure is an attitude, not a place. Get up and keep crawling, sliding, and falling forward in the direction of your dreams. If you follow the hero's path, eventually you will get there.

Chapter 15:

Establishing Customer Relations Through Effective Communication To Maximize Profits

"One cannot always oblige; one can, however, always speak obligingly" says Sri Sathya Sai Baba, Indian spiritual master, which is an exact explanation for the complex role of corporate communication in modern corporations today.

The customer, as the old saying goes, is the king! A king he truly is he believes, that is, till the not-so-charitable mandarins of marketing let him know and make him aware, rather painfully for him, that he is one among the many millions that feel that way, without actually being that way. However, the same mandarins grudgingly acknowledge that a happy customer is a brand's success, while a delighted customer is a brand's ambassador. The customer relationship management paradigm - popularly abbreviated as CRM - is built precisely on these pillars. And the customer enjoys a precarious position in this paradigm.

In the concentrated CRM efforts, a company often forgets the basic thing that is the cornerstone of the concept... relationship! Traditional marketing theories have always focused on attracting new customers, rather than retaining existing customers. Over the past decade, thanks to intensified competition and greater variety of products, this has gradually altered. The current flavor of marketing is 'retain' more than 'gain'. Because retention leads to growth and growth leads to fulfillment.

In marketing, today, the consumer is treated not as a king but like a mischievous sprite. He is accused - well, almost - of making a brand dance to his wishes and whims. While purists tend to argue that brands need customers and vice versa, modernists counter it by saying that customers need a brand, any brand, so long as the brand is his willing genie. This disproportionate balance shapes brand communication strategies. Positioning per se is no longer a marketer's tool but rather as an awkward proposition to grab the customer's fancy. Positioning is not brand or product or benefit or feature-centric anymore; it is customer-centric.

What is then important to establish a relationship between a brand and its customer? In order to build a personal relationship, the brand's personality has to come through (Michael C Gray, 2006). It will no longer be brand and customer, but simply 'you' and 'I'... a collaboration is well-developed leads to 'we', which could be a fulfilling state for a brand and a customer.

Social researchers have always advised marketers that people prefer to do business with people, not institutions or brands. This implies that corporate communication has to be the link that helps to build and maintain a healthy relationship between both stakeholders. Technically there can be several types of regular communication: newsletters, fax messages, voice broadcasts, blogs, sales letters, emails and more.

Communication with customers reflects the following aspects of a relationship.

- Strong culture
- Favorable identity
- Coherent philosophy
- Genuine sense of camaraderie

It may not be instant gratification or affection but effective corporate communication establishes an appropriate and professional relationship with the customer, including quick, responsible channels of two-way communication. Corporate Communication is all about managing perceptions and ensuring that with effective and timely dissemination of information a positive corporate image is created that ensures a smooth and affirmative relationship with all customers, at all times.

Be it a corporate body, company, research institution, non-governmental organization, PSU, all of them need to have a respectable image and reputation in the eyes of the customer. In today's day and age of increasing competition, easy access to information and media explosion - reputation management has gained even greater importance. So, corporate communications as a role has become significant and professional in nature while dealing with customers.

Gone are the days when corporate communications merely meant 'wining and dining the client'; it has now emerged as a science and art of perception management. The concept of managing relationships with customers is as old as trade itself, but the focus has always been to sell products and services (Kotler, Philip, Introduction to Marketing Principles). Competition, driven by globalization and, the Internet have changed the face of business. Customers now have a variety of choices and, most importantly, they are becoming far more knowledgeable and demanding. The power has truly shifted to the customer. With this scenario, most companies realize that they need to treat their customers with more care.

Companies are now desperately searching for different ways to manage their relationships effectively, not only to acquire new customers, but also to retain the existing ones. According to a Harvard Business Review Study by Reicheld & Sasser, some companies can boost their profits by almost 100% by retaining just 5% or more of their existing customers.

Customers express their satisfaction in many ways. When they are satisfied, they mostly say nothing but return again, and again, to buy or use more. Measuring satisfaction is only half the story.

It is also necessary to determine customers' expectations or the importance they attach to different overtures of a brand, otherwise resources could be spent raising satisfaction levels of things that do not matter. The measurement of expectations or importance is more difficult than the measurement of satisfaction. Many people do not know or cannot admit, even to themselves, what is important.

Consumers do not spend their time rationalizing why they do things, their views change and they may not be able to easily communicate or admit to the complex issues in the buying argument. A customer satisfaction index is a snapshot at a point in time. People's views change continuously and the performance of companies in delivering customer satisfaction is also changing. Measuring satisfaction must be a continuous process.

Even when experts discuss CRM, the discussion is almost always from the point of view of marketing, sales and business development. Seldom is CRM looked upon as a 'goal' that every organization should actively pursue. Often it is looked upon as a tool that every organization could use. The differences are plenty. And CRM is not an IT function. CRM is more often a function of communication, by the company directly, through an intermediary such as a PR agency or simply through the media.

Successful CRM practices is not about statistics, data warehousing or loyalty programs, rather it is about competing in the relationship dimension-not as an alternative to having a competitive product or reasonable price-but acting as a differentiator in terms of 'feelings for the customer', however, abstractly - and sometimes absurdly - romantic that may sound. If brands can get an edge based on how customers feel about the brand, it's a much more sustainable relationship in the long run. This feeling for a brand, as brand theorists prefer to call it is directly proportional to the communication efforts, written words and spoken sentences, that emanate from a company.

Link it to the corporate communication strategy and you will have a direct connect between the company and its customer. The critical dimension of any CRM practice is the relationship that a brand shares with its customers. Using the word customer itself may sound a trifle improper here because 'customer' implies that the person is 'outside' a relationship. And any relationship is expressed and nurtured by communication.

Almost always marketers try to understand a customer from the marketing perspective, as people who have to be 'given' something to retain their loyalty. This naturally places them on a moral (and commercial) pedestal that enables them to look down upon hapless customers as beneficiaries of their largess. In communication parlance this signifies up and down power positions. And in a relationship between equals the power position is not hierarchical. Sometimes the anachronistic social mindset refuses to place the customer on even keel with a brand - and vice versa - painting him as a king, or as an unrealistically greedy pauper.

CRM is a simple process, because establishing a relationship is simple. No where is understanding more profound than when it comes to human emotions... but surprisingly the very same human emotions have been overlooked by companies while interacting with their customers.

What is a relationship? When is there a relationship between two entities? What is the role of corporate communications in establishing, maintaining and fulfilling such relationships? Relationship could simply mean to be a particular type of connection existing between people related to with each other biologically or emotionally and having social or economic dealings with each other. Unfortunately, all pretenses of dealing with relationships that often ask for simplicity, empathy, credibility and sincerity cease the moment commercial returns on investments are discussed. Which is what communication is all about; communicating to customers, and not with them.

Researchers have often argued that to understand brand-customer relationships, it is necessary to consider what the brand thinks of its customers, more than what the customers think of a brand. Marketers struggle hard to enhance the satisfaction of customers only to find that they choose their competitors. Why does this happen? Research has further shown that investments in customer communication, which logically seems to be the most crucial aspect in a relationship, has been the most neglected area in most companies.

The argument for this lies in the reality that 65% of all customer service activities are outsourced to business processing units (BPUs). That means the brand does not directly handle customer interactions and queries - unless they are of a certain level, of course. This is akin to asking your friend to talk to your representative about everything that you want to say, including... affairs of the heart, and speak directly only if it is something serious! This attitude, in the first instance, is marketing-driven and one-sided. There are also many brand loyalty programs, which are being attempted by marketers in isolation without the back up support of several other relevant and related strategies. There is a distinctive need for marketers to understand the importance of customer communication, and not merely look at it from the point of view of PR, Advertising or other known corporate forms of communication.

Often corporate communication strategies are designed... to work as a bridge between stakeholders, to justify policies and decisions, to deliver business strategies, to inform and persuade, and of course to emphasize that the company is committed to putting customer interests first, almost as an afterthought!

Thus corporate communications is almost always understood as a process used to build, foster, nurture and extend business relationships with customers. This is unfortunately a bureaucratic understanding, as GE's former CEO Jack Welch says, "Bureaucracies love to focus inward. It's not that they dislike customers; they just don't find them as interesting as themselves." And the communication reflects it.

In 'Customers Are People: The Human Touch', author Jon McKean states that in competitive markets, where customers have a choice between similar products and pricing, "70% percent of customer decision-making is based on how customers are treated." "Yet," McKean adds, "Over 80 per cent of customer initiatives are focused on 'selling to customers better' through superior products, prices and promotions, than in investing more resources in treating customers better..." How best can a person be treated? By simply being talked to in a better manner.

The question staring squarely on the faces of companies is: "How to make a customer loyal?" When companies talk of relationships where customers have real choices, they are honestly trying to be the best suitor to the customer, 'as the customer sees it', and not 'as they want the customer to see it'. Reichheld and other loyalty experts have studied this issue for years and have concluded that relationships are driven by the behaviour and perception of customers of the value of the relationship that exists between the brand and himself, which is the net result of what economic and psychological value the customer receives from the brand.

According to psychologists customers' emotional states influence about 50 percent of the value they perceive from their purchases. Jim Barnes, author of 'Secrets of Customer Relationship Management: It's All About How You Make Them Feel', sums it up by saying, "Value is created every time a customer is made to feel welcome, important and valued."

After reasonably agreeing to the fact that the important aspects in CRM are relationship and how customers, on account of their distinct behaviour and personality, differently and uniquely perceive a relationship, it is also imperative to stress on the point that corporate communication is the prime driver of any relationship. As the leading Indian telecom brand AirTel shows in its advertisements, communication is all about expressing oneself.

A brand identity is shaped by a collective interactive experience of customers, product, policy, and strategy. Which is why developing a brand-customer relationship is important. The choice is simple: either a brand makes a customer experience or it gets created despite the brand. To create a successful relationship, the brand must develop a compelling identity with the customer and have a genuine value proposition. The brand must rely on customer perspective, appreciate the viewpoint and have the ability to communicate appropriately. A common pitfall for many brands is that they do not take the time to think how they should articulate the brand identity. Needless to say, a successful brand strategy is incomplete without a sound communications strategy. The organization must be aligned in ways that anticipate and fulfill customers' emotional expectations at every touch point to create meaningful relationships and lasting competitive advantage.

Successful customer communication clearly highlights the brand's functional, emotional, and self-expressive benefits, as the customer would like to see. It is delivered in a way that is superior or unique when compared to competitors. Customer experience is shaped by a series of interactions with an organization.

According to Jonathan Hardcastle, barriers to effective communication such as frames of reference, value judgments, selective listening, filtering and distrust (all between sender and receiver) complicate the communication systems and messages. However, these can be overcomed by sending clear, complete, and specific messages, which are to put it rather romantically, 'straight from the heart'. Demonstrating love and affection, clarifying intentions, being reliable and dynamic can enhance credibility, exhibiting warmth and friendliness, and building a positive image. Soliciting and providing specific feedback can also enhance communication effectiveness between partners, which is what brands should consider customers as.

One of the most important consumer satisfaction elements is the ability to ask questions and being able to receive appropriately satisfying answers from the brand's representatives. Gaining information, uncovering motives, giving incentives, obtaining participation, checking understanding, initiating the thinking process, inducing agreements, and refocusing attention, are all essential components of an effective consumer communication plan. Thus, the active listening skills of a brand help to build rapport with customers that is both intimate and empathetic.

The other most important aspect is the subtle non-verbal communication of a brand and the customers, that is useful both in reading the underlying emotions and attitudes of customers, while reinforcing a brand's verbal messages. Understanding subtle communication can enhance the brand-customer relationship.

Coupled with this are improving standards of technology and devices that add an edge to the communication process. Unfortunately over-dependence on technology and automation has had an adverse impact on customer relationship. While on one hand brands talk of a relationship - a concept normally associated with living things largely and human beings in particular - on the other hand, the overuse of technology has led to a dissociation that has taken the customer and brand away from each other. This dichotomous situation has to be recognised by the brand as well as the customer, for communication is all about power positions, and it is important to understand that in a relationship the power positions are on an even keel.

Concluding, due to the growing complexity and turbulence of the business environment and the related growth in research knowledge about customer behavior patterns, managers of the 21st century have to take four themes as paramount; the necessity of managing the challenges of change; functioning within a global environment; being sensitive to the diversity among people; and behaving with ethical integrity.

The final ingredient that binds a customer to your brand in a lasting relationship is dialogue. Your company's brand isn't a monolithic, hermetic face that the organization presents to the world. Rather, it's an ongoing exchange where you listen carefully to your customers, understand what they say, and respond by modifying your value proposition and extending your businesses appropriately to fulfil customers' desires. You exist because of the customer. This selflessness is the cornerstone to successful CRM.

Therefore any corporate communication effort should focus broadly on three aspects: understanding relationships, understanding the distinct behaviour of consumers to relationship overtures and understanding (and establishing) the role of communication in effective and enduring customer relationships.

CONCLUSION

Conclusion and Business valuation

There are 3 approaches to valuing a business – market, income and asset. A thorough business valuation requires that you consider methods from all approaches. Each valuation method looks at a company from a different perspective, and sometimes the results vary widely. How do you choose the best method?

Selecting Methods The asset-based method described in produces the minimum value of a company because it assigns no value to goodwill. So, your first step is to ignore any method that produces a value less than the adjusted asset method. If your company has little or no earning capacity then the adjusted asset method may produce the highest result and it is the best method.

The percentage of annual sales method from often produces the highest value of a company because it is based on top-line sales only and it ignores gross profits and operating expenses. Because it produces a high value many owners latch on to this method even though it often produces unrealistic results.

Since the primary driver of business value is earning capacity, the multiple of seller's discretionary earnings (SDE) and capitalized cash flow methods tend to produce the most realistic values. On the flip-side, potential buyers and their lenders will also be looking at earnings to justify the selling price.

Range of Values

Typically the adjusted asset method will be the lowest, the percentage of annual sales method will be the highest, and the SDE and cash flow methods will fall somewhere in-between. This is the range of values for your company. Because valuation is based on a hypothetical sale of your company, the value of your company depends upon the most likely terms of the sale. If you had to sell fast for all cash then you would probably sell near the low end. If you had time and were willing finance a significant portion of the selling price then you are likely to sell closer to the top. Under normal circumstances, the value of your company will fall near the middle.

Limitations

No matter how much time and effort you put in to valuing your company, you will never be able to match the training and experience of a valuation professional.

In addition to expertise, a valuation professional brings another critical factor to the process - objectivity. There are many judgment calls made during the valuation process. No matter how objective you may have been in doing your valuation, your objectivity will still be subject to reasonable doubt.

Your lack of valuation experience and questionable objectivity means that your self-prepared valuation will hold little weight with outside third parties. Doing your own valuation only makes sense if you are going to use the results for your own personal or business purposes. Basing a major decision or course of action on the results of a self-prepared valuation is not a good idea. The impact of using an off-the-mark value may cost you many times the cost of hiring a valuation professional.

On the other hand, your self-prepared valuation will be better than many of the free or low-cost valuation services available **online.**

Conclusion

Doing your own business valuation using the instructions in this guide will produce a result that will give you a good idea of what your company is worth. During the valuation process, you will learn more about your company, and what drives its value. At that point, you will know more about your business than most owners, and will be able to manage it more effectively.

Good job on reading the entire book! Finally, if this book provided any value for you, a review on Amazon would be appreciated!

Flip to the next pages for more books like this.

Two book package deal

Whether you are ready to start your business or not, it is always a wise decision to create extra sources of passive income. Investing in stocks or real estate can potentially generate thousands and even tens of thousands of dollars every month with very little or no effort at all once you know how to do it. This two-book package is going to give you a head start and teach you what you need to know to start investing today!

"Search "Passive Income By Mark Atwood" at amazon.com. to preview the book"

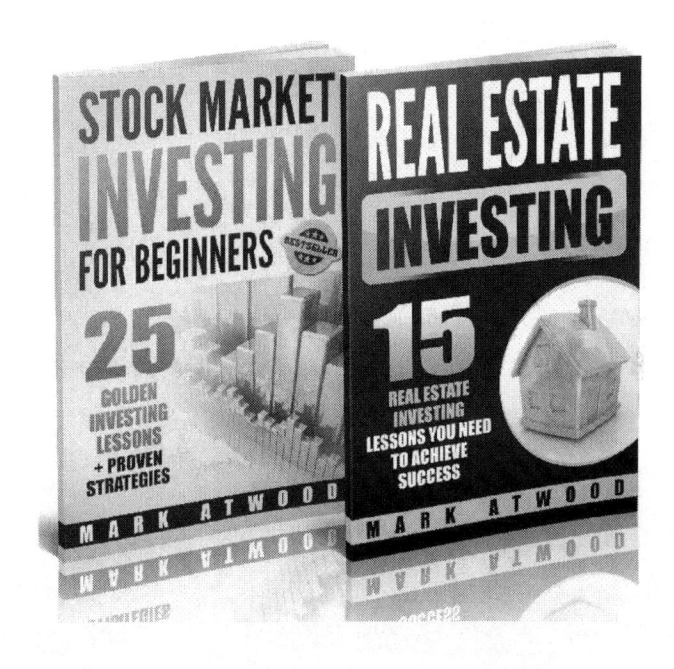

Not sure what kind of business to start? This book gives you 25 proven online-business ideas that you can start today!

"Search "Passive Income By Mark Atwood" at amazon.com. to preview the book"

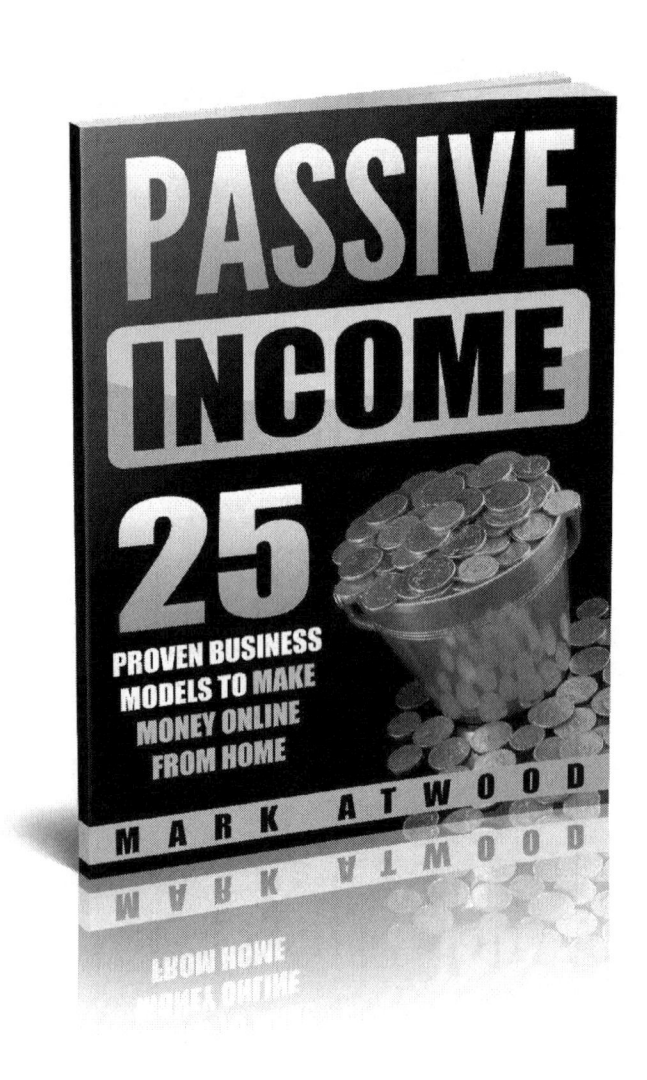

Made in the USA
San Bernardino, CA
14 May 2019